PREFACE

I FIRST HEARD about the relationship between blood moons, the feasts of Israel, and the end times in the early fall of 2008 at a prophecy conference. During his presentation, one of the other speakers presented the view that a coming "blood moon" (lunar eclipse) that fell in close proximity to the Jewish Feast of Tabernacles signaled the soon coming of the Lord. Careful not to be labeled a date setter, the presenter constantly hedged his bets, yet he all but said this was a harbinger of the end or that the even more significant blood moon occurrence in 2014–2015 would signal the end.

Then, in October 2013, I had the privilege to speak at the largest annual prophecy conference in the United States, and questions about the relationship between the four blood moons in 2014–2015 came up several times in the question-and-answer session and while talking to individuals.

About the same time, John Hagee's book *Four Blood Moons* was released, becoming an instant bestseller. By the time this book is published, Mark Biltz will have released his book *Blood Moons: Decoding the Imminent Heavenly Signs*. In 2007 Pastor Biltz first discovered the correlation between when blood moons fell on Jewish feast days and key historical world events involving the Jewish people. He claimed to have found the divine link or intersection between biblical prophecy, historical events, and heavenly signs.

Being a student of Bible prophecy, I was of course interested, so I watched several videos of Mark Biltz's teaching about the blood moons prophecy and the Jewish feasts and read *Four Blood Moons* to learn what the furor was all about. I agree with many things in John Hagee's *Four Blood Moons* about God's future plan for national Israel, the Rapture, the Second Coming, and our need to be ready at any time for the Lord's return. I also deeply appreciate his commitment to the Jewish people and passion to bless them, in keeping with Genesis 12:1-3. Yet when it comes to his analysis of the four blood moons and their relationship to Scripture, history, and the end times, I disagree with his interpretation of some Scriptures and the conclusions he draws from the historical data. My view is that much of what people are saying today about blood moons is based on speculation and a misinterpretation of Scripture.

Blood Moons Rising will examine in the light of Scripture the view that many well-known prophecy teachers are presenting. In this book I will disagree with fellow believers, but my disagreement is not intended to be personal. I appreciate others who give their lives to ministry for Christ and His body, and I don't claim to have it all figured out when it

BLOOD MOONS RISING

BLOOD

BIBLE PROPHECY, ISRAEL, AND

MOONS

THE FOUR BLOOD MOONS

RISING

MARK HITCHCOCK

Tyndale House Publishers, Inc., Carol Stream, Illinois

Visit Tyndale online at www.tyndale.com.

TYNDALE and Tyndale's quill logo are registered trademarks of Tyndale House Publishers, Inc.

Designed by Dean H. Renninger

Published in association with the literary agency of William K. Jensen Literary Agency, 119 Bampton Court, Eugene, Oregon 97404.

Library of Congress Cataloging-in-Publication Data

Hitchcock, Mark, date.
  Blood moons rising : Bible prophecy, Israel, and the four blood moons / Mark Hitchcock.
    pages cm
  Includes bibliographical references.
  ISBN 978-1-4143-9708-5 (sc)
  1. End of the world. 2. Moon—Religious aspects—Christianity. I. Title.
  BT877.H56 2014
  236´.9—dc23   2014002037

Printed in the United States of America

20   19   18   17   16   15   14
7

The history of the world is about to change forever, and God is sending us messages on His high-definition billboard by speaking to us in the heavens—using the Four Blood Moons; the question is . . . are we listening? . . .

The next Tetrad will end in September 2015, which will include the Year of Shemittah. Will a crisis happen as before? What earthshaking event will it be? This we know: things are about to change forever! . . .

The Shemittah year and Feast of Tabernacles begin at sunset September 25, 2014. These occurrences are not coincidental! This is the hand of God orchestrating the signs in the heavens. The final Four Blood Moons are signaling that something big is coming . . . something that will change the world forever.

—JOHN HAGEE, *FOUR BLOOD MOONS: SOMETHING IS ABOUT TO CHANGE*[1]

TABLE OF CONTENTS

Preface *ix*

CHAPTER 1 The Final Four? *1*

CHAPTER 2 Setting the Stage *13*

CHAPTER 3 The End-Times Script *27*

CHAPTER 4 Dark Side of the Moon *55*

CHAPTER 5 Seven Feasts and Four Blood Moons *69*

CHAPTER 6 Moonshine: Signs in the Heavens *91*

CHAPTER 7 Blood Moons and Bible Prophecy *103*

CHAPTER 8 Once in a Blood Moon *127*

CHAPTER 9 The Dating Game *139*

CHAPTER 10 Blood Moons and You *157*

APPENDIX 1 Leviticus 23: The Feasts of the Lord *171*

APPENDIX 2 Foreshadows of the Future *179*

APPENDIX 3 A Proposed Chronology of the End Times *189*

Notes *197*

comes to end-times prophecy. When I disagree, I hope to do so in an irenic spirit.

My goal is to present what I believe Scripture says about the end times, examine the historical evidence for the blood moons prophecy, and leave you to make your own decision. I used to be an attorney, so I want to make my case, present the evidence, and let you render your own verdict.

My prayer is that the Lord will use this book to help bring greater clarity about what lies ahead as we await the coming of the Lord, and stir within each heart a readiness for that day.

Mark Hitchcock
EDMOND, OK
JANUARY 2014

Chapter One

THE FINAL FOUR?

What a time to take the news of the day in one hand and the Bible in the other and watch the unfolding of the great drama of the ages come together. This is an exciting and thrilling time to be alive. . . . It is not just Christians that sense something is about to happen. The world knows that things cannot go on as they are. History has reached an impasse. This world is on a collision course. Something is about to give. With increasing frequency, commentators from secular media speak of Armageddon.

—BILLY GRAHAM, *THE REASON FOR MY HOPE*[1]

IN A *PEANUTS* comic strip, Snoopy is sitting on his doghouse, typing a novel. He begins his story the way he always begins his stories, with the words "It was a dark and stormy night."

Lucy comes by and puts in her two cents. In her assertive, blunt way, she scolds him: "That's a terrible way to begin a story. It's so trite! 'Once upon a time . . .' that's the way all the good stories begin." Lucy lectures him more and then leaves.

The last frame of the comic shows Snoopy starting over on his story. This time he types, "Once upon a time, it was a dark and stormy night."

Snoopy's first line is an apt description of how many feel today. It's a dark and stormy night. The constantly escalating tempo of life in combination with cataclysmic natural disasters, wars and rumors of wars, unrest in the Middle East, terrorism, and mushrooming financial uncertainty have given the entire world a sense of impending crisis. People today are asking questions about the future as never before—solemn, searching questions. Apocalypse is in the air. Many have a sense that the world is nearing closing time, that a day of reckoning is at hand. The words of philosopher Alfred North Whitehead are truer than ever: "It is the business of the future to be dangerous."[2]

Some are taking drastic steps to get ready. Doomsday preparation is booming. Plans for surviving nuclear fallout, the shifting of the earth's crust, complete financial meltdown, or the final apocalypse have reached new heights, or even new depths. The Vivos Survival Shelter & Resort in Atchison, Kansas, for example, is the world's largest private underground shelter. The developers are converting an enormous underground limestone mine that covers 135 acres into square footage equal to the Empire State Building (2.25 million square feet). The luxury doomsday bunker has enough food and water to provide for five thousand people for a year.[3] Many others are also taking precautions, albeit on a smaller scale.

Science fiction writer Arthur C. Clarke observed, "This is the first age that's paid much attention to the future, which is a little ironic since we might not have one."[4] Recent polls reflect the growing sentiment that something big is about to happen and that the end of the age is approaching:

- "Almost one in three Americans see Syria's recent conflict as part of the Bible's plan for the end times."
- "One in four think that a U.S. military strike in Syria could lead to Armageddon."

- "Nearly 15 percent of people worldwide believe the world will end during their lifetime."
- "41 percent of all U.S. adults, 54 percent of Protestants, and 77 percent of evangelicals believe the world is now living in the biblical end times."
- "Nearly 4 in 10 Americans (and 65 percent of white evangelicals) believe recent natural disasters are evidence of the End Times."[5]

Hollywood reflects the mood of the mob. The apocalypse is big business. Hollywood is churning out television series and movies based on postapocalyptic scenarios. Richard Swenson notes how things have changed in recent times: "Before the nuclearization of the modern era, much of the literature of science fiction dealt with the promise of a glorious technological future. Today such optimism is seldom seen. Forty years ago, Hollywood's futuristic movies were utopian. Now they are all apocalyptic."[6] Here are a few recent examples.

- *The Book of Eli* (2010)
- *The Road* (2009)
- *Revolution* (2012)
- *Elysium* (2013)
- *Oblivion* (2013)
- *This Is the End* (2013)
- *World War Z* (2013)
- *The World's End* (2013)

- *2012* (2009)
- *The Walking Dead* (2010)
- *Falling Skies* (2011)

In recent times attempts to forecast the end have increased with predictions such as John R. Gribbin and Stephen H. Plagemann's *The Jupiter Effect*; Michael Drosnin's *The Bible Code, The Bible Code II: The Countdown*, and *The Bible Code III: Saving the World*; the panic surrounding Y2K and the year 2000; renewed interest in the quatrains of Nostradamus; and more recently the end-of-the-world predictions surrounding December 21, 2012. Following mystic Mayan prophecies, predictions of the end of the world were all over the Internet in the years leading up to 2012. While many predicted the end of the world, some in the New Age movement heralded the dawning of a new day for mankind in December 2012—an age of Aquarius. Nothing happened, which shouldn't surprise us. History is strewn with the bleached bones of prophecies and predictions that have failed the test of time.

While Hollywood and false prophets consistently miss the mark concerning the future, many signs that we see around us do point toward the end-times scenario laid out in Scripture. The Jewish people are back in their ancient homeland after a worldwide dispersion of almost two thousand years, just as Scripture predicted thousands of years ago. Peace in the Middle East is under constant negotiation, and the Middle East is center stage. Globalism and exponential advances in technology have provided the framework for the end-times global government and economy predicted in Revelation 13. Israel sits surrounded by a sea of enemies who would delight in its destruction. Russia and Iran have risen to prominence as predicted in Ezekiel 38–39, along with other Islamic nations that despise Israel. Events in our world strikingly foreshadow the biblical predictions of the end of the age. We live in the times of the signs. End-times biblical prophecies will be fulfilled right on time on God's calendar, just as hundreds of past prophecies have been fulfilled.

MOON SHADOW

Jesus said that in the days before His return there will be stunning signs on earth (see Matthew 24:4-28) and in the heavens (see Luke 21:25). Other biblical prophets predicted celestial signs in the heavens of Christ's second advent. Based on these prophecies, a growing number of prophecy teachers today maintain that an astronomical event in 2014–2015 is a dramatic sign in the heavens that is about to change everything—that something very big is coming that will change the world forever.

The specific astronomical sign they point to is known as a "tetrad," which is the appearance of four blood moons (lunar eclipses) falling on two Jewish feast days or high holy days (Passover and the Feast of Tabernacles). It's known as the blood moons prophecy. This view is spreading quickly, and people everywhere are asking questions about its significance. The central question is this: Is the blood moons prophecy different from all the apocalypse forecasts we have seen before? Is this another prophecy miscalculation, or could this celestial event be the most incredible sign of the times the world has ever witnessed?

According to NASA, four blood moons will appear on four Jewish feast days in 2014–2015. In the middle of the sequence, there will be a solar eclipse. Here are the times of their appearance.

BLOOD MOONS OF 2014-2015	
04/15/2014	Passover
10/08/2014	Feast of Tabernacles
03/20/2015	Total Solar Eclipse
04/04/2015	Passover
09/28/2015	Feast of Tabernacles

These total lunar eclipses are known as blood moons because when they occur, the moon takes on a reddish hue or blood color. Many prophecy teachers, based on three past occurrences of this phenomenon and a few prophetic Scriptures that mention the moon turning to blood, believe that this tetrad of blood moons signals some impending event in Israel and America or even the end of the age. They believe this could be the *final four*.

John Hagee, the pastor of Cornerstone Church in San Antonio, has championed this view in his recent bestselling book *Four Blood Moons*. Hagee's teaching is substantially derived from Mark Biltz of El Shaddai Ministries, who was the first to discover the alleged blood moons prophecy. He appears in numerous videos on the Internet and has authored a book titled *Blood Moons: Decoding the Imminent Heavenly Signs*. But John Hagee, with his worldwide television audience, has popularized the view and taken it mainstream. He believes that something dramatic, even world changing, is about to happen. He writes in *Four Blood Moons*:

> This is the hand of God orchestrating the signs
> in the heavens. The final Four Blood Moons
> are signaling that something big is coming . . .
> something that will change the world forever. But
> the bigger question is, are we watching and listening?
> . . . What they *are* telling us is that God is getting
> ready to change the course of human history once
> again. He is preparing to display the next series of
> signs in the heavens. What is going to happen?[7]

Some are saying the blood moons are a sign of war involving Israel in 2015. Michael Snyder notes, "According to ancient Jewish tradition, a lunar eclipse is a harbinger of bad things for Israel. If that eclipse is blood red, that is a sign that war is coming. And blood red moons that happen during Biblical festivals seem to be particularly significant."[8]

I watched John Hagee on Trinity Broadcasting Network on November 1, 2013, when he appeared with a panel of prophecy experts to say that if America doesn't repent, something drastic will occur in 2015. He didn't give any specific indication of what he expects, but he alluded to an event like the World Trade Center attack on September 11, 2001, or the economic collapse of 2008. Hagee bases his prediction on the fact that every seven years in Israel was to be a Sabbatical year, or Shemittah, when Israel was to allow the land to rest and not plant crops. When Israel neglected this provision in the Law, there was judgment. God exiled the Jewish people to Babylon for 70 years for failing to observe the Sabbatical year for 490 years (see 2 Chronicles 36:20-21).

Hagee applies this to America and notes that the year 2001 was a Shemittah year, and 9/11 happened. Seven years later, in 2008—another Shemittah year—the economic tsunami hit America and the world, bringing the global economy to its knees. Adding seven years to 2008 brings us to 2015. Hagee asks the question:

> Will America be at war? Will America's mountain
> of debt come crashing down, destroying the dollar?
> Will global terrorists attack our nation again with a
> force that will make 9/11 pale by comparison?
> The attacks on the Twin Towers were on
> September 11, 2001.
> The Wall Street crash was on September 29,
> 2008.
> The next Tetrad will end in September 2015,
> which will include the Year of Shemittah. Will a
> crisis happen as before? What earthshaking event will
> it be?

This we know: things are about to change forever![9]

Hagee and others who hold to the blood moons prophecy are forecasting a national cataclysm if America fails to repent.

THE SEARCH FOR ANSWERS

Four blood moons will appear in 2014–2015 and will fall on two Jewish feasts in each year—that much we know for sure. As this phenomenon bears down on planet Earth, a growing number of people are asking serious questions and even making predictions, and I expect the predictions and anxiety to increase dramatically in 2015. But what's it all really about? What's the uproar? Is there any truth to the notion that these blood moons portend ominous events for Israel, for America, and possibly even for the world? People everywhere are asking questions. Inquiring minds want to know. Is there about to be some great change or shift as some claim? Is the apocalypse upon us? The questions we face today are very real.

- Does the Bible say anything about blood moons?
- Are the four blood moons a *harbinger* or *hype*?
- Are they *signs* or *sensationalism*?
- Will America face judgment in 2015?
- Is the world racing toward Armageddon?
- Is there hope for the future?

In the pages that follow I hope to answer these questions and more as we consider what the Bible says about Israel, blood moons, and the end of days.

Chapter Two

SETTING THE STAGE

. . . .

As students of the Bible observe proper interpretation principles, they are becoming increasingly aware of a remarkable correspondence between the obvious trend of world events and what the Bible predicted centuries ago.

—JOHN F. WALVOORD, *ARMAGEDDON, OIL,*
  AND THE MIDDLE EAST CRISIS[1]

SOME SIGNS ARE easier to read than others. If you have ever traveled to a foreign country, you know that all too well. Meaning quickly gets lost in translation. Consider these translated signs in other countries:

- In a Paris elevator: "Please leave your values at the front desk."
- In a Hong Kong supermarket: "For your convenience, we recommend courageous, efficient self-service."
- In a Rhodes tailor shop: "Order your summers suit. Because is big rush we will execute customers in strict rotation."
- In a Hong Kong tailor shop: "Ladies may have a fit upstairs."
- In Kyushi, Japan, on a Detour sign: "Stop: Drive Sideways."
- In a Copenhagen airline ticket office: "We take your bags and send them in all directions." (Yes, they do!)

• In an Acapulco hotel: "The manager has personally passed all the water served here."[2]

Most of us have experienced miscommunication like this. Some signs are simple, straightforward, and easy to read, while others are a bit more difficult. The same is true when it comes to signs of the times. They are often misunderstood and misapplied.

Many today present the blood moons prophecy as a significant sign of the times—an omen of coming events. For this reason, before we delve into the details related to the four blood moons and their alleged significance as signs of the end times, I want to give a very brief definition and discussion of what prophetic signs of the times are to make sure we all know what we're talking about.

SIGN ME UP

What are prophetic signs of the times? Are they important? Should we be looking for them? How do they relate to what's coming? Simply stated, prophetic signs of the times are current events that foreshadow future events predicted in the Bible. Signs of the times are like signs on the highway: they point toward or herald what's ahead. They indicate what's coming. Signs of the times are not fulfillments of prophecy per se but are events that indicate the future fulfillment of prophecy. When it comes to understanding or discerning signs of the times, there are three basic approaches.

Approach #1: Skepticism

Many today believe it's foolish and speculative to even consider signs of the times. They argue it's a colossal waste of time and energy and an unnecessary distraction since no one knows the time of the Lord's coming. They grow weary and even cynical of talk of the end times. The apocalypse has been predicted for millennia, yet we're still here. Skeptics also correctly point out times in the past when extremists have set dates for end-times events or made other reckless predictions that never materialized. (I'll discuss this later, in chapter 9.) Skepticism seriously questions or even outright rejects any notion of signs of the end times. Many Christians today fall into this category.

Those who belong to this camp often accuse those who believe in signs of practicing "newspaper exegesis," which Thomas Ice and Timothy Demy explain as "human ideas, not the Bible, [being] the true source of such beliefs, such that they arise from a search of newspaper headlines rather than from exegesis (i.e., proper interpretation) of the biblical text."[3] Certainly, skeptics are correct that some of this occurs, but I don't believe all signs of the times should be discounted because of a few reckless teachers.

Approach #2: Sensationalism

At the other end of the spectrum, some view almost everything as a stirring sign of the times. Richard Swenson writes, "Hysteria brings fire to the eyes and acid to the stomach. Hype brings notoriety. Sensationalism brings a tabloid kind of success."[4] Sensationalists are like that old song: "Sign, sign, everywhere a sign." Every earthquake, natural disaster, crime wave, war, new advance in technology, or rumble in the Middle East is touted as an earth-shattering sign that Jesus is coming soon. For sensationalists, signs are everywhere and almost everything. In some circles, wild speculation is far too common and most often is not based on sound principles of biblical interpretation.[5]

While there are several problems with a sensational approach to signs of the times, one practical problem is that when almost everything becomes a sign, then nothing is a sign. If everything is a sign, then the entire notion of signs becomes meaningless. Extreme, unfounded prophetic speculation often discredits the Bible, gives biblical prophecy a black eye, and should be denounced by all responsible, thoughtful believers.

Approach #3: Stage-Setting

The mediating view that I adopt is often called *stage-setting*. This view maintains that the events of the end times cannot occur in a vacuum. There has to be some buildup, setting of the stage, or paving the way before end-times events unfold. We look at future events predicted in the Bible, and when current events dramatically correspond to or strikingly point toward the biblical template, these stage-setting events serve as discernible signs of the times. We don't read the Bible in light of the headlines, but we *do* read headlines in light of Bible prophecy.

Using this guideline, we can track general trends in preparation for the end times.

In the time before the first coming of Christ, God arranged the world for His Advent. The world was prepared religiously, linguistically, and politically for the birth of Jesus. Galatians 4:4 says, "When the fullness of the time came, God sent forth His Son, born of a woman, born under the Law." Dr. John Walvoord says, "Just as history was prepared for Christ's first coming, in a similar way history is preparing for the events leading up to His Second Coming. . . . If this is the case, it leads to the inevitable conclusion that the Rapture may be excitingly near."[6]

Another way to understand signs of the times is that we can observe the end-times scenario in Scripture and reverse engineer it to the events that must precede that scene and pave the way for its arrival. Thomas Ice and Timothy Demy say,

> The Bible provides detailed prophecy about the seven-year tribulation. In fact, Revelation 4–19 gives a detailed, sequential outline of the major players and events. Using Revelation as a framework, a Bible student is able to harmonize the hundreds of other biblical passages that speak of the seven-year tribulation into a clear model of the next time period for planet earth. With such a template to guide us, we can see that already God is preparing or setting the stage of the world in which the great drama of the tribulation will unfold.[7]

Ice also says, "Just as many people set their clothes out the night before they wear them the following day, so in the same sense is God preparing the world for the certain fulfillment of prophecy in a future time."[8]

Another key to understanding and confirming stage-setting as an approach to signs of the times is the current convergence of so many signs in a short period of time. Skeptics often point out that there have always been events touted as signs of the times. So what's different today? Are we just repeating the overreaction and shortsightedness of previous generations who thought they saw signs of the Lord's coming in their time? I don't think so. The convergence and acceleration of so many events is what leads me to believe that the end-times stage is being set today. Since the rebirth of Israel in 1948, and even more in the last twenty years, things in our world seem to be on fast-forward. With 24-7 worldwide news coverage and global means of communication, events in our world have immediate, almost exponential impact. So many events are converging in such a brief window that I cannot ignore them and pass off the convergence as coincidence. Richard Swenson highlights the "generational shift" our world is experiencing, which I believe is driving the setting of the world stage:

The fundamentals have changed. Life pace and change are escalating wildly. Without our permission, history has picked up speed, turbo-charged by progress. Add in the powerful cofactors of technology and information, mix it with abundant economic "gunpowder," and you have cooked up a nice cocktail of exponential explosiveness. The locomotive guiding history jumped the tracks, and instead of traveling down the local-stop commuter spur, it switched to supersonic status. Instead of chugging, it now explodes out of the station, breaking the sound barrier before it even leaves the gate.[9]

Dr. John Walvoord echoes such a belief concerning current stage-setting in preparation for prophetic fulfillment: "More prophecies have either been fulfilled or prepared for fulfillment in our day than in all the previous centuries since the first of our era. . . . The preparation for the final drama is being carried on before our eyes."[10]

One final point I want to emphasize as strongly as I can is that stage-setting is *not* date setting. I believe that no one knows the time of any end-times event, not the decade, the year, the month, or the day. No one knows how long it will take for God to get things ready, but the convergence and acceleration of signs should stir a sense of urgency in our lives.

JESUS AND SIGNS OF THE TIMES

Jesus Himself spoke of signs of the times. In Matthew 16:2-3 Jesus answers the request of the Pharisees and Sadducees for a sign from heaven: "When it is evening, you say, 'It will be fair weather, for the sky is red.' And in the morning, 'There will be a storm today, for the sky is red and threatening.' Do you know how to discern the appearance of the sky, but cannot discern the signs of the times?" Jesus was speaking in these verses of the signs of His first coming as Israel's Messiah. Jesus fulfilled the Old Testament prophecies about the coming of the Messiah and chided the people in His day for failing to discern the signs of the times.

Later, Jesus shifts from the focus on His first coming and gives a long list of specific signs of His second coming (see Matthew 24:4-29). Luke 21:25 records the words of Jesus Himself saying that cosmic signs will portend His return to earth. Clearly, Jesus believed in signs of the times—signs for His first coming and signs of His return.

Hebrews 10:24-25 also seems to support the notion of signs of the times: "Let us consider how to stimulate one another to love and good deeds, not forsaking our own assembling together, as is the habit of some, but encouraging one another; and all the more as you see the day drawing near." The "day drawing near" in the context of the book of Hebrews is the day of the Lord's coming. If we cannot see the day drawing near, then this verse makes no sense. Signs of the times point toward the coming of Christ. Of course, no one knows how long the buildup or stage-setting will last until our Lord returns. It could be days, months, or years—maybe even many years.

One important distinction to keep in mind is that signs of the times relate to the second coming of Christ, not the Rapture. We will talk more about these two events in the next chapter, but I believe the Rapture is the next event on

God's prophetic calendar. It can happen at any moment. The second coming of Christ to earth will occur at the end of the seven-year Tribulation and will be signaled by numerous signs, as Jesus said in Matthew 24. If we can already see the signs of the Second Coming, but the Rapture (which precedes it) hasn't happened yet, then the Rapture could be very soon. One way to understand how signs relate to the Lord's coming is to think of Christmas and Thanksgiving. Signs of Christmas are everywhere in the fall, sometimes beginning as soon as September or early October. You can't miss the signs for Christmas. The Second Coming is like Christmas. Thanksgiving is another matter. There really aren't any clear signs of Thanksgiving. The Rapture is like Thanksgiving—it's a signless event. Yet if you can see the signs of Christmas, and Thanksgiving hasn't arrived, you can be sure that Thanksgiving is near. In the same way, if we can already see the buildup for the Second Coming today, then we can know the Rapture could be very soon. It could be today. Christ can come to rapture us to heaven at any time.

THREE MAIN VIEWS OF SIGNS OF THE TIMES
Skepticism: There are no signs of the times.
Sensationalism: Almost everything is a sign.
Stage-Setting: Some major developments in our world today are discernible signs of the end times.

The setting of the world stage for future, end-times events can be illustrated by picturing a theater where preparations are made for a production.[11] Suppose a seasoned drama critic enters a theater one evening not knowing which of Shakespeare's masterpieces is to be presented. Before the curtain goes up, he is taken behind the scenes. Onstage is a castle with fortifications looking out over a wooded countryside. At once he knows that he will not see *Othello*, which is set in Venice, or *Julius Caesar*, which begins with a street scene in Rome. He knows he will not see *Macbeth* because although there is a castle scene in *Macbeth*, the play opens not with the castle but with witches gathered around their cauldron. Finally, our drama critic notices two soldiers with shields bearing the arms of the king of Denmark. He sees two other actors dressed as a king and a queen. There is an actor who is supposed to be a ghost. No one has to tell the critic what he will see. Based on his knowledge of Shakespeare and the clues he has seen, he knows it will be *Hamlet*.

In the same way today, God's people sit in the theater of world events awaiting the curtain call of God's apocalyptic drama. We don't know when the play will begin, but like the drama critic, we know much more about it than most. Many stare at the future as at a huge curtain. For them the future is veiled because they have no idea of the plan of God. And they can't see behind the curtain where act one is being set. For believers, however, we see behind the scenes. While it is true that we don't know the moment when the play will begin, we do know the play itself—the main characters and events—and can sense it beginning as we see the actors starting to take their places on the great world stage.[12]

In 1974, John Walvoord, in his bestselling book *Armageddon, Oil, and the Middle East Crisis,* wrote these classic words that are more relevant today than when he wrote them:

> Our present world is well prepared for the
> beginning of the prophetic drama that will lead
> to Armageddon. Since the stage is being set for
> this dramatic climax of the age, it must mean that
> Christ's coming for His own is very near. If there
> ever was an hour when men should consider their
> personal relationship to Jesus Christ, it is today. God
> is saying to this generation: "Prepare for the coming
> of the Lord."[13]

That's the key message for our day.

Chapter Three

THE END-TIMES SCRIPT

· ·

If you want to know what happened yesterday, read the newspaper; if you want to know what happened today, listen to the evening news; if you want to know what will happen tomorrow, read the Bible.

—ANONYMOUS

I LIKE THE story of the man who approaches a beach and sees a woman in the water with a huge shark fin bearing down on her. Panicked, he yells, "Shark! Shark!" But the people sitting on the beach in chairs don't move. Nobody does anything. Thinking they can't hear him, he sprints toward the beach, keeps hollering, and wildly waves his arms. As he gets closer to the beach, he sees a man sitting in a chair with the word *DIRECTOR* on the back. He'd come upon the scene of a movie shoot. What had looked to him like danger and chaos was all under the control of a director.

It's often the same for us. We look at this world and see mounting chaos and confusion and are tempted to panic. As someone has observed, "There are three days a week that we have no control over—yesterday, today, and tomorrow." But we have to remember it's all under the control of a Divine Director. He wrote the script, He's calling the shots, and He's directing every detail so that it will all play out as He has planned. Nothing happening in our world takes God by surprise. There's never any panic in heaven. The Trinity never has to meet in emergency session. God has it all under control.

My favorite word in biblical prophecy is a name for God in the book of Revelation—the Almighty. The English word *Almighty* is a translation of the Greek word *Pantokrator*, which literally means to have everything in your hands or to have your hands on everything. God Almighty is the One who has His sovereign hands on everything, including the future of this universe and your future. He's directing everything in accordance with His eternal purposes.

PREVIEW OF COMING ATTRACTIONS

To make sure we have our bearings before we get into the specifics of the blood moons prophecy, I want to take you on a flyover—a view from thirty thousand feet—of the future prophetic landscape presented in Scripture, a big-picture panorama of the end-times drama that God has written and is directing. I believe that knowing God's prophetic blueprint for the future will help us keep things straight as we look at some of the specific events in more detail later in this book.

As we peek behind the curtain, we see ten key events that will shape everything that happens in the future—ten events that acquaint us with the main characters and events of the end times. Understanding what's coming provides the biblical framework or mirror for events today that serve as true signs of the times.

Event #1: The Regathering

The most prophesied event in end-times passages in the Bible is the return of the Jewish people to their Promised Land. The Bible predicts over and over again that the Jews must be back in their homeland for the events of the end times to unfold (see Jeremiah 30:1-3; Ezekiel 34:11-24; 37:1-28; Zechariah 10:6-10). Almost all the key events of the end times hinge in one way or another on the return of the Jewish people and the existence of the nation of Israel. The tiny land of Israel is the stage for all the great end-times wars and conflicts in Scripture. The Jewish people must be preserved and regathered to their ancient homeland for end-times biblical prophecy to be fulfilled.

I believe the end times officially begin when the Antichrist makes a seven-year treaty with Israel (see Daniel 9:26-27). In order for this to happen, Israel must exist. Ezekiel 38–39 and Zechariah 12 describe military invasions of the nation of Israel in the end times. Again, for these prophecies to be literally fulfilled, the Jewish people must be back in their land.

The United Nations approved a national homeland for the Jews, and British control of the land ended on May 14, 1948. The new nation was given five thousand square miles of territory and had a population of 650,000 Jews and several hundred thousand Arabs. Further waves of immigrants have poured into Israel from all over the world.

For the first time since AD 135 there are now more Jews in Israel—almost six million—than in any other place on earth. According to Haaretz.com, "The data indicates the closure of an historical circle: For the first time since the destruction of the Second Temple, Israel has once again become the largest concentration of Jews in the world."[1] To put this in perspective, in 1948 only 6 percent of the Jews in the world were in Israel. Today, it stands at almost 40 percent. By the year 2030 it is estimated that half of the Jews worldwide will be back in the land. Prophetically, the process and preparation over the last 130 years are staggering. For the first time in two thousand years the Jews have returned and continue to come home to their land—just as the ancient prophets predicted.

The number one sign of the times, and the monumental miracle of the twentieth century, is the return of the Jewish people to their homeland from worldwide dispersion and exile. And we are the generation that has a front-row seat to see it happen. We are witnessing what believers in former generations only dreamed of. This points toward the fulfillment of other key end-times prophecies.

Israel today is the nation at the center, just as the Bible predicted for the end times. Israel is the fuse for the powder keg of the final world conflict. The end-times script cannot be acted out until Israel is back in her land. Israel is the fulcrum of the future. According to Daniel 9:27, the seven-year Tribulation can't even start until Israel is back in the land and willing to make peace with the final world ruler. The fuse is moving into place for the first time in almost two thousand years. This is the *supersign* of the end times, paving the way for other prophetic signposts to line up along the road to Armageddon. As Adrian Rogers says, "These are dangerous days in which we live! The storm clouds are gathering. The lightning is flashing—and the lightning rod is Israel. Christians cannot deny or ignore the significance of the nation of Israel."[2]

Event #2: The Vanishing

Someday, any day—perhaps even today—the world will be shocked by the Rapture of the church, the sudden removal of every Christian from the world. This event, which will traumatize and change the world forever in an instant, is prophesied in 1 Thessalonians 4:13-18:

> We do not want you to be uninformed, brethren, about those who are asleep, so that you will not grieve as do the rest who have no hope. For if we believe that Jesus died and rose again, even so God will bring with Him those who have fallen asleep in Jesus. For this we say to you by the word of the Lord, that we who are alive and remain until the coming of the Lord, will not precede those who have fallen asleep. For the Lord Himself will descend from heaven with a shout, with the voice of the archangel and with the trumpet of God, and the dead in Christ will rise first. Then we who are alive and remain will be caught up together with them in the clouds to

meet the Lord in the air, and so we shall always be with the Lord. Therefore comfort one another with these words.

A further description is found in 1 Corinthians 15:50-53:

I say this, brethren, that flesh and blood cannot inherit the kingdom of God; nor does the perishable inherit the imperishable. Behold, I tell you a mystery; we will not all sleep, but we will all be changed, in a moment, in the twinkling of an eye, at the last trumpet; for the trumpet will sound, and the dead will be raised imperishable, and we will be changed. For this perishable must put on the imperishable, and this mortal must put on immortality.

This shocking event will fulfill the reassuring promise of Christ to His disciples on the night before He died, when He said, "Do not let your heart be troubled; believe in God, believe also in Me. In My Father's house are many dwelling places; if it were not so, I would have told you; for I go to prepare a place for you. If I go and prepare a place for you, I will come again and receive you to Myself, that where I am, there you may be also" (John 14:1-3).

When the Lord comes for His people at the Rapture, the bodies of Christians who have died will be resurrected and rejoined with their perfected spirits, and every true Christian alive on earth will instantaneously be transported to heaven without experiencing death. They will do an end run on the grave.

I believe the Rapture is the next great event on God's prophetic calendar and could happen at any moment. There's nothing that *must* occur for the Rapture to take place. It's an event that is certain to occur, but when it will occur is uncertain. Like the big earthquake everyone is expecting on the US West Coast. Everyone knows it will come, but no one knows when. No signs or warnings must precede it. It can strike at any moment. The same is true of the Rapture. We are constantly living on the edge of eternity. We need to live each day on "ready."

As you can imagine, the Rapture will dumbfound the world. Picture the immediate, instantaneous disappearance of millions of people all over the globe. For half the world it will be night. Beds will be emptied, or in some cases one will be taken and one left behind. For the other half of the world, there will be unfathomable, indescribable chaos: driverless cars, pilotless planes. People from all walks of life will suddenly vanish without a trace, except a pile of clothes with watches, jewelry, glasses, and dentures (or even more replacement parts). The vanishing of millions of Christians will deepen the religious, political, and economic confusion already present in the world, paving the way for power to fall into the hands of the religious, political, and economic opportunists waiting in the wings.

Event #3: The Reuniting

In the aftermath of the Rapture and the inevitable chaos, people will desperately search for answers, for someone to bring some order out of the confusion. The Bible teaches that ten leaders, what we might call the "Group of Ten," will rise from the area of the historic Roman Empire. We could describe them as a ruling oligarchy or controlling committee.

The ten leaders are symbolized by the ten toes of Nebuchadnezzar's metallic image in Daniel 2:41-44, the ten horns of the frightening beast in Daniel 7:7, and the similar description of the end-times government in Revelation 13:1 and 17:12-14.

The coalition or confederacy of ten leaders and the nations they represent constitutes a revival or reuniting of the Roman Empire and signals the final stage of the fourth beast in Daniel 7. The Group of Ten will rise to power to protect Western interests and to guarantee the peace and security of the Middle East (and possibly to guarantee the continued supply of oil). These goals will be temporarily solidified in a seven-year covenant of peace and protection with Israel (see Daniel 9:27). As you can imagine, unless peace is imposed, chaos, disruption of the precious oil supply, and an escalation in terrorism could threaten to bring Western civilization to its knees. The current twenty-eight nations of the European Union appear to encompass the emergent stage of this final world power.

Event #4: The Calming

Modern Israel was born on Friday, May 14, 1948. But the nation's birth was accompanied by serious complications. At its birth, Israel was attacked by six surrounding nations who virulently opposed the establishment of the Jewish state. From that day until today, Israel has remained in a state of war with most of its Arab neighbors (except for Egypt and Jordan, but even that could change at any time with the recent developments in Egypt). Israel's neighbors stubbornly refuse to even acknowledge its existence.

All attempts at lasting peace in the Middle East have failed miserably. People everywhere wonder, and probably doubt, if there will ever be enduring peace in the region. Yet, incredibly, the Bible predicts that a temporary time of peace will sweep the world, especially the Middle East, as a prelude and staging ground for end-times events. This period of peace is described by the apostle Paul in 1 Thessalonians 5:1-3:

> As to the times and the epochs, brethren, you have no need of anything to be written to you. For you yourselves know full well that the day of the Lord will come just like a thief in the night. While they are saying, "Peace and safety!" then destruction will come upon them suddenly like labor pains upon a woman with child, and they will not escape.

According to Scripture, the terrible time of tribulation will catch the world totally off guard. The world will be basking in the sunlight of peace, albeit temporarily. This portrait of peace, especially in the Middle East, seems so distant and inconceivable today. How in the world will Israel ever reach a point when it feels secure enough to let down its guard? Daniel 9:27 provides the biblical answer: "He will make a firm covenant with the many for one week, but in the middle of the week he will put a stop to sacrifice and grain offering; and on the wing of abominations will come one who makes desolate, even until a complete destruction, one that is decreed, is poured out on the one who makes desolate."

The "he" in verse 27 refers back to "the prince who is to come" in verse 26—the coming world ruler or final Antichrist who rises alongside the Group of Ten. From the swarm of negotiators and advisers involved in the Middle East, one striking international leader will emerge from the reunited Roman Empire to superimpose a peace settlement on Israel and its militant neighbors, putting an end to the chaos in the Middle East and assuring the flow of oil to the West. According to Daniel 9:27, the treaty commences the final seven years of this age.

Revelation 6:1-2 further highlights this coming peace: "I saw when the Lamb broke one of the seven seals, and I heard one of the four living creatures saying as with a voice of thunder, 'Come.' I looked, and behold, a white horse, and he who sat on it had a bow; and a crown was given to him, and he went out conquering and to conquer." The rider on the white horse is the final Antichrist who enters the global scene as a great peacemaker. He counterfeits the true Christ, who will ride a white horse at His glorious coming (see Revelation 19:11). Antichrist's rise will usher in a brief era of false peace and pave the way for his one-world government and global economy.

This mirrors what we see today. The only possible hope for the Middle East is a durable, enforceable, comprehensive imposed peace initiative. We can see today how this prophecy could be fulfilled very soon. The world is crying out for peace. The yearning for peace in the Middle East is the number one foreign policy and diplomatic issue of our day. The Bible predicted this event 2,500 years ago. A time of calm is coming, but it will only be the calm before the storm.

Event #5: The Invading

In the wake of the peace agreement and its guarantee of security, Israel will let down its guard for the first time in modern history. Seeing this vulnerability and their chance to strike, Russia, Iran, and several Islamic nations will devise a plan to storm Israel and at the same time deal a decisive blow against the Western leader who has guaranteed Israel's peace by means of the seven-year treaty (see Ezekiel 38:1-11).

This end-times conflict is called the Battle of Gog and Magog. Activated by animosity for Israel and jealousy over her abundant prosperity (possibly including recent discoveries of massive oil and gas fields), the Russian-Islamic coalition will storm Israel in a major surprise attack at some point during the first half of the Tribulation.

Event #6: The Deifying

When Russia, Iran, and their allies launch their final power grab in the Middle East against Israel, God will supernaturally intervene to annihilate the invaders. The crushing defeat is graphically presented in Ezekiel 38:18-23:

> "It will come about on that day, when Gog comes against the land of Israel," declares the Lord GOD, "that My fury will mount up in My anger. In My zeal and in My blazing wrath I declare that on that day there will surely be a great earthquake in the land of Israel. The fish of the sea, the birds of the heavens, the beasts of the field, all the creeping things that creep on the earth, and all the men who are on the face of the earth will shake at My presence; the mountains also will be thrown down, the steep pathways will collapse and every wall will fall to the ground. I will call for a sword against him on all My mountains," declares the Lord GOD. "Every man's sword will be against his brother. With pestilence and with blood I will enter into judgment with him; and I will rain on him and on his troops, and on the many peoples who are with him, a torrential rain, with hailstones, fire and brimstone. I will magnify Myself, sanctify Myself, and make Myself known in the sight of many nations; and they will know that I am the LORD."

Needless to say, this event will dramatically reshape world geopolitics in the end times. With the annihilation of Russia and her Islamic allies, the balance of power will swing decisively to the world's new strongman—the Antichrist. As Satan's man of the hour, he will seize the opportunity and attempt to destroy Israel, now disarmed and at peace. To further project his powerful persona, he may even take credit for the destruction of the Russian-Islamic army. In an act of daring brashness and blasphemy, he will deify himself and command the worship of the world (see 2 Thessalonians 2:4; Revelation 13:4, 8).

His henchman, known as the beast out of the earth or the false prophet, will institute a passport for commerce or Tribulation trademark that all will be forced to take or die. This "mark of the beast," or 666, will constitute a pledge of allegiance to the Antichrist—a taking of his name upon the right hand or forehead (Revelation 13:16-18). This final period of three and a half years, when Antichrist rules the world politically, economically, and religiously, will be the terrible time Jesus identified as the "great tribulation" (Matthew 24:21).

Event #7: The Judging

The seven-year Tribulation will include a series of almost inconceivable catastrophes outlined in Revelation 6–19. Three successive series of seven judgments will rock the world—seven seals, seven trumpets, and seven bowls.

Acts of man—resulting in thousands of martyrs—and acts of God will combine to cause great disturbances on earth and in the heavens. Stars will fall, and planets will run off course, causing chaotic changes in climate (see Revelation 6:13-14; 16:8-9). Global heating and cooling, flooding, and other disasters will decimate much of the food production of the world (see Revelation 6:6-8). Famine will grip the world, causing millions to perish (see Matthew 24:7). Pandemic plagues will sweep the world, killing millions (see Revelation 6:6-8). As this period miserably grinds to a close, earthquakes will level the great cities of the world, and geological upheavals will cause mountains and islands to sink into the seas (see Revelation 16:17-20). Disaster after disaster will shrink world population in the course of a few years to a fraction of its present billions.

Revelation 6–16 is the main section of the Bible that describes the end-times Tribulation. These eleven chapters focus upon the awful judgments of the end times. The main thread running through these chapters is the three sets of seven judgments that the Lord pours out on the earth: seven seal judgments (Revelation 6), seven trumpet judgments (Revelation 8–9), and seven bowl judgments (Revelation 16). These series of judgments will be poured out chronologically or successively during the Tribulation.

The seven seals will be opened during the first half of the Tribulation. Their effect will reverberate throughout the entire seven years, but they will begin during the first three and a half years of the Tribulation. The seventh seal contains seven trumpets, which will be blown during the second half of the Tribulation. The seventh trumpet unleashes the seven bowls or vials that will be poured out in a very brief period of time right near the end of the Tribulation, just before Christ returns.

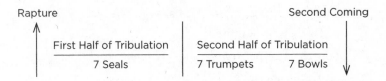

These pounding judgments are often compared in Scripture with birth pangs (see Jeremiah 30:4-7; Matthew 24:8; 1 Thessalonians 5:3). Like birth pangs, these judgments will irreversibly intensify in their severity and frequency as the Tribulation progresses.

These three crashing waves of God's judgment are described in detail in Revelation 6–16.

SEVEN SEAL JUDGMENTS

- First Seal (6:1-2): White Horse—Antichrist
- Second Seal (6:3-4): Red Horse—War
- Third Seal (6:5-6): Black Horse—Hyperinflation and Famine
- Fourth Seal (6:7-8): Pale Horse—Death and Hell
- Fifth Seal (6:9-11): Martyrs in Heaven
- Sixth Seal (6:12-17): Universal Upheaval and Devastation
- Seventh Seal (8:1-2): The Seven Trumpets

SEVEN TRUMPET JUDGMENTS

- First Trumpet (8:7): Bloody Hail and Fire—One-Third of Vegetation Destroyed
- Second Trumpet (8:8-9): Fireball from Heaven—One-Third of Oceans Polluted
- Third Trumpet (8:10-11): Falling Star—One-Third of Freshwater Polluted
- Fourth Trumpet (8:12): Darkness—One-Third of Sun, Moon, and Stars Darkened
- Fifth Trumpet (9:1-12): Demonic Invasion—Torment
- Sixth Trumpet (9:13-21): Demonic Army—One-Third of Mankind Killed
- Seventh Trumpet (11:15-19): The Kingdom—The Announcement of Christ's Reign

SEVEN BOWL JUDGMENTS

- First Bowl (16:2): Upon the Earth—Sores on the Worshipers of the Antichrist
- Second Bowl (16:3): Upon the Seas—Turned to Blood
- Third Bowl (16:4-7): Upon the Freshwater—Turned to Blood
- Fourth Bowl (16:8-9): Upon the Sun—Intense, Scorching Heat
- Fifth Bowl (16:10-11): Upon the Antichrist's Kingdom—Darkness and Pain
- Sixth Bowl (16:12-16): Upon the River Euphrates—Armageddon

- Seventh Bowl (16:17-21): Upon the Air—
  Earthquakes and Hail

It boggles our minds just to read this list. One-half of the earth's population perishes in just two of the nineteen judgments (see Revelation 6:8; 9:18).[3] The earth's environment will be destroyed. Revelation 16:19-21 graphically depicts the worldwide devastation: "The cities of the nations fell. . . . And every island fled away, and the mountains were not found. And huge hailstones, about one hundred pounds each, came down from heaven upon men."

Just think what it would be like to miss the Rapture and live on earth while all this is transpiring. The world will teeter on the brink of destruction.

Event #8: The Fighting

Culminating this series of divine judgments will be a world war of unprecedented proportions. Hundreds of millions of troops from all over the world will gather for a gigantic world power struggle centered in the land of Israel at a place called Armageddon (see Revelation 16:13-16). In today's culture, the term *Armageddon* has come to describe anyone's worst fear of the end of the world or of any great catastrophe, but its real meaning is much more specific. Found only one time in Scripture, the word *Armageddon* refers to the final suicidal war, a desperate death struggle, centered in the northern part of Israel.

The name *Armageddon* actually comes from a Hebrew word meaning "the Mount of Megiddo," a small mountain located in northern Israel at the end of a broad valley that is fourteen miles wide and twenty miles long. The Valley of Jezreel or Valley of Megiddo has been the scene of many military conflicts in the past and will be the focal point of this great future conflict. The area will become the scene of the greatest war of history. Great armies from all over the world will pour into Israel for the final military showdown. Locked in this lethal struggle, millions will perish. This final, shattering, history-ending war will occur in the exact place predicted in Scripture and right on time according to God's schedule. We can see the signposts on the road to Armageddon lining up in today's headlines.

Event #9: The Coming

When the armies gathered at Armageddon see the sign of Christ's coming, they will foolishly turn their hatred against Him (see Revelation 19:19). Man's stubborn rebellion against Christ will reach its apex, but resistance will be futile. Jesus Christ will come back in power and glory from heaven, escorted by millions of angels and raptured Christians. The greatest event in human history is vividly described in Revelation 19:11-21:

> I saw heaven opened, and behold, a white horse,
> and He who sat on it is called Faithful and True,

and in righteousness He judges and wages war. His eyes are a flame of fire, and on His head are many diadems; and He has a name written on Him which no one knows except Himself. He is clothed with a robe dipped in blood, and His name is called The Word of God. And the armies which are in heaven, clothed in fine linen, white and clean, were following Him on white horses. From His mouth comes a sharp sword, so that with it He may strike down the nations, and He will rule them with a rod of iron; and He treads the wine press of the fierce wrath of God, the Almighty. And on His robe and on His thigh He has a name written, "KING OF KINGS, AND LORD OF LORDS." Then I saw an angel standing in the sun, and he cried out with a loud voice, saying to all the birds which fly in midheaven, "Come, assemble for the great supper of God, so that you may eat the flesh of kings and the flesh of commanders and the flesh of mighty men and the flesh of horses and of those who sit on them and the flesh of all men, both free men and slaves, and small and great." And I saw the beast and the kings of the earth and their armies assembled to make war against Him who sat on the horse and against His army. And the beast was seized, and with him the false prophet who performed the signs in his presence, by which he deceived those who had received the mark of the beast and those who worshiped his image; these two were thrown alive into the lake of fire which burns with brimstone. And the rest were killed with the sword which came from the mouth of Him who sat on the horse, and all the birds were filled with their flesh.

Returning as the King of kings and righteous Judge of the world, Jesus will destroy the fighting forces at Armageddon by the word of his mouth (see 2 Thessalonians 2:8; Revelation 19:15). There really won't be a battle at all. As one of my seminary professors used to say, "All Jesus will have to do is say, 'Drop dead,' and it will all be over!" The gathered forces will be slain, and the beast and false prophet will be cast alive into the lake of fire (see Revelation 19:20-21).

Event #10: The Reigning

After His enemies are destroyed, Jesus will order the binding of Satan in the abyss so that Jesus can establish His glorious Kingdom of peace and righteousness on earth for a thousand years, which is often referred to as the Millennium (see Revelation 20:1-6). God's original purpose for creation and mankind will be fulfilled on a restored, renewed earth under the gracious rule of the Messiah. Man's perpetual, unsatisfied longing for true peace and prosperity will finally be realized under the rule of the King of kings.

As Billy Graham says, "A fabulous future is on the way. The second coming of Christ will be so revolutionary that it will change every aspect of life on this planet. Christ will reign in righteousness. Disease will be eliminated. Death will be abolished. War will be eradicated. Nature will be transformed. Men, women, and children will live as life was originally designed, in fellowship with God and each other."[4] This is man's only hope.

At the end of the thousand years, Satan will be released for a short time for one final stand, only to be crushed and cast into the lake of fire forever (see Revelation 20:7-10). The final judgment of all the lost will then occur at the great white throne, with Jesus presiding as supreme Judge (see Revelation 20:11-15).

The crescendo of God's work will be the creation of a new heaven and new earth. The old order will be dismantled and destroyed and replaced by a new universe and new earth (see Psalm 102:25-27; Matthew 24:35; 2 Peter 3:10-14; Revelation 21:1-9). The heavenly city, the new Jerusalem— the dwelling place of God—will come down to sit on the new earth. Like a floating continent—a 1,500-mile cube— the city will serve as the capital city or metropolis of the new universe (see Revelation 21:10–22:5). God's people will dwell with Him, "and they will reign forever and ever" (Revelation 22:5). Paradise will be eternally restored and regained.

You might want to pause here for a moment to take all this in and make sure you have digested this basic timeline, because you'll see some of these terms sprinkled throughout this book. But more important, this is the future of the universe. This is the future of everyone reading these words! We are all part of God's great plan—either enjoying salvation or facing judgment. Consider where you stand with the Lord. He is the God of judgment, but He is also the God of grace and salvation through Jesus Christ.

PUTTING THE PIECES TOGETHER

The key to putting together a puzzle is the picture on top of the box. You look at it to put the pieces in place. The same is true with the prophetic puzzle. The picture on the top of the box is the prophetic picture set forth in God's Word. Our world today is looking more and more like the picture on top of the box all the time. The prophetic picture is taking shape before our eyes.

The world stage is being set. The buildup is before us.

We live today in what is often called the church age, the time when God is saving Jews and Gentiles all over the world and forming us together into the church, the body of Christ. The Rapture can happen at any time, ending this present age and igniting God's end-times drama.

As we wait for the Rapture, people everywhere seem to have the foreboding sense that a storm is on the horizon. The Middle East is the focus of the world just as the Bible has said it will be in the end. Israel is a powerful nation in a sea of enemies. The desperate cry for peace in the Middle East is unrelenting. The nations of the Roman Empire are re-forming. Dramatic changes in the Middle East point toward an all-out war with Israel. Globalism makes the rule of one man over the entire earth possible for the first time in human history. All the necessary preparations are falling into place. The signposts are lining up. The groundwork is being laid. Like pieces on a chessboard or actors on a theater set, the nations are taking their predicted places. Ancient prophecies will be fulfilled just as literally as the ones that have already come to pass. The world rushes headlong to its destiny set forth in the pages of Scripture.

MAJOR EVENTS OF UNFULFILLED PROPHECY

1. Rapture of the church	John 14:1-3; 1 Corinthians 15:51-58; 1 Thessalonians 4:13-18
2. Reuniting of the Roman Empire under a group of ten leaders	Daniel 7:7, 24; Revelation 13:1; 17:3, 12-13
3. Jewish temple rebuilt in Jerusalem	Daniel 9:27; 12:11; Matthew 24:15; 2 Thessalonians 2:4; Revelation 11:1-2
4. Rise of the Antichrist	Daniel 7:8; Revelation 13:18
5. Signing of the seven-year peace treaty with Israel	Daniel 9:27
6. Russia, Iran, and Islamic allies spring a surprise attack on Israel	Ezekiel 38–39
7. Peace treaty with Israel broken after three and a half years; beginning of one-world government, one-world economy, and one-world religion	Daniel 7:23; Revelation 13:5-8, 15-17; 17:16-17
8. Mark of the beast (666) established as a pledge of allegiance to the Antichrist and as a passport for doing business	Revelation 13:16-18
9. Many Christians and Jews martyred who refuse to worship the world dictator and receive his mark	Revelation 7:9-17; 13:15

MAJOR EVENTS OF UNFULFILLED PROPHECY	
10. Catastrophic, global divine judgments and environmental disasters represented by seals, trumpets, and bowls poured out on the earth in succession	Revelation 6–16
11. World war breaks out, focused in the Middle East: campaign of Armageddon	Revelation 16:12-16
12. City of Babylon, an end-times headquarters of Antichrist, is destroyed	Revelation 17–18
13. Second coming of Christ	Matthew 24:27-31; Revelation 19:11-21
14. Judgment of unbelievers living on earth when Christ returns	Ezekiel 20:33-38; Matthew 25:31-46; Jude 1:14-15; Revelation 19:15-21; 20:1-4
15. Satan bound in the abyss for a thousand years	Revelation 20:1-3
16. Resurrection of Tribulation saints and Old Testament saints	Daniel 12:2; Revelation 20:4
17. Millennial (thousand-year) kingdom and reign of Christ begins	Revelation 20:5-6
18. Final satanic rebellion at the end of the Millennium	Revelation 20:7-10
19. Resurrection and final judgment of the unsaved (unbelievers): Great White Throne Judgment	Revelation 20:11-15
20. Eternity: new heaven, new earth, new Jerusalem	Revelation 21:1-2[5]

Chapter Four

DARK SIDE OF THE MOON

· ·

The sun will be turned into darkness

And the moon into blood

Before the great and awesome day

of the LORD comes.

—JOEL 2:31

A PASSENGER IN a taxicab leaned forward to ask the driver a question, and while doing so, he tapped him on the shoulder. The driver screamed, lost control of the taxi, nearly hit a bus, and drove over the curb before coming to a stop inches from a shop window. For a moment everything was silent in the cab until the shaken driver finally said, "I'm really sorry, but you scared the living daylights out of me!" The startled passenger apologized and said he didn't realize that tapping him on the shoulder would frighten him like that. The driver replied, "No, it's not your fault. Today is my first day driving a cab—I've been driving a hearse for the past twenty-five years."

People nowadays are jumpy and fearful about many things, whether it's the stock market, the housing market, the job market, the insurance market, or the supermarket. When we throw in other concerns like terrorism, crazy weather patterns, and crime, there are plenty of things to keep us on edge. But all these things are faint shadows compared to the coming events that will rock this world.

Events in our world today are unfolding just as we should expect in light of biblical prophecy. More and more, our times mirror the biblical image of the end times set forth in Scripture. As we have discussed, these events that point toward what's coming are often called "signs of the times." The central question before us in this book is, what are the signs that portend the Lord's coming? Or more specifically, do the four blood moons in 2014–2015 play a part in God's plan? Are they the final four? Are they a signal that something is about to change?

WHAT IS A BLOOD MOON?

Before we dive into the details of answering these questions and others, we need to understand a few basic things about blood moons. First, we need to establish a basic definition of a blood moon. A blood moon is the result of a total lunar eclipse. According to NASA,

> a lunar eclipse occurs when the Earth lines up directly
> between the sun and the moon, blocking the sun's
> rays and casting a shadow on the moon. As the moon
> moves deeper and deeper into the Earth's shadow, the
> moon changes color before your very eyes, turning
> from gray to an orange or deep shade of red.
>
> The moon takes on this new color because

indirect sunlight is still able to pass through Earth's atmosphere and cast a glow on the moon. Our atmosphere filters out most of the blue colored light, leaving the red and orange hues that we see during a lunar eclipse.[1]

With this understanding in mind, let's consider the blood moons theory promoted by Mark Biltz, John Hagee, and others. The blood moons theory is built upon four main ideas. First, God uses the heavens to give signs to humanity. Second, science confirms there will be four blood moons in 2014–2015, falling on the Jewish feasts of Passover and Tabernacles. Third, Scripture mentions the moon turning to blood in conjunction with the end times. And fourth, history reveals that when four blood moons fell on Jewish feasts in the past five hundred years, significant events transpired involving the Jewish people and/or their land.

SIGNS IN THE HEAVENS

The foundation for God's using the heavens to give signs to humanity is Genesis 1:14: "God said, 'Let there be lights in the expanse of the heavens to separate the day from the night, and let them be for signs and for seasons and for days and years.'" Hagee believes that "signs" means "signals," that the heavens serve to give direction to mankind.[2] Mark Biltz emphasizes that the words "signs" and "seasons" refer to appointed times, such as the Jewish feasts.

Luke 21:25, 28 are used to further support the notion of signs in the heavens. Jesus says, "There will be signs in sun and moon and stars, and on the earth dismay among nations, in perplexity at the roaring of the sea and the waves. . . . But when these things begin to take place, straighten up and lift up your heads, because your redemption is drawing near."

From Genesis 1:14 and Luke 21:25, 28, proponents of the blood moons prophecy argue that God uses the heavens as "His divine billboard announcing coming events."[3] The billboards in the heavens are where God advertises what He's about to do. Blood moons are believed to be a key part of God's heavenly signal to man that something ominous is on the horizon.

While the vast majority of biblical prophecy teachers agree that God uses cosmic signs as precursors of end-times events, the question is, does the Bible specifically identify four blood moons as a heavenly sign of coming events?

MOONSTRUCK

Another prong of the argument for the blood moons prophecy comes from science. This point is simple and straightforward. Astronomy confirms that four blood moons will occur in 2014–2015, falling on the two Jewish feasts of Passover and Tabernacles in succession.

Astronomers can predict the appearance of comets, lunar and solar eclipses, and various conjunctions of planets and stars because of the staggering consistency and precision of the universe. Like a cosmic clock, more accurate than any timepiece on earth, the heavens move with a symmetry and schedule that points to our great Creator. As Richard Swenson says, "The universe is a vast, rich, and beautiful place. It is both comforting and fear-inspiring. Every molecule and every magnetar speak of God. 'The universe,' said Thomas Carlyle, 'is but one vast symbol of God.'"⁴

Part of the precision of God's creation is the predictability of lunar eclipses or blood moons. According to astronomers, two blood moons will appear in 2014. Consider the detail of the prediction:

> The night of April 14 and into the early hours
> of April 15 there will be a total lunar eclipse. . . .
> Astronomers in North and South America will
> best be able to view this eclipse, which should last
> for 75–80 minutes. . . . On October 8 the second
> total lunar eclipse of the year will occur, visible to
> the western half of North America, Hawaii, eastern
> Asia, Indonesia, New Zealand and the eastern half of
> Australia. Across central and eastern North America
> the moon will set while entirely covered by Earth's
> shadow. This eclipse is expected to last one hour.⁵

Likewise, in 2015, two lunar eclipses will be visible. The eclipse on April 4, 2015, "will be visible in Asia, Australia, Pacific and the Americas with a duration of 3h 29m. Of this time the eclipse will be total for 5m." The blood moon on

September 28, 2015, "will be visible in Asia, Australia, Pacific and the Americas with a duration of 3h 20m. Of this time the eclipse will be total for 1h 12m."[6]

Four blood moons are certain. All agree on this point. The issue is, what prophetic significance, if any, does this phenomenon hold? Does it mark a sudden shift along the prophetic fault line that will change everything?

LUNAR LIGHT

Another pillar for the blood moons theory is an appeal to Scripture. Five main biblical passages refer to signs in the moon related to the end times. I've emphasized the reference to the moon in each passage.

> I will display wonders in the sky and on the earth, blood, fire and columns of smoke. The sun will be turned into darkness and *the moon into blood* before the great and awesome day of the LORD comes. (Joel 2:30-31)

> Immediately after the tribulation of those days THE SUN WILL BE DARKENED, AND *THE MOON WILL NOT GIVE ITS LIGHT*, AND THE STARS WILL FALL from the sky, and the powers of the heavens will be shaken. And then the sign of the Son of Man will appear in the sky, and then all the tribes of the earth will mourn, and they will see the SON OF MAN COMING

ON THE CLOUDS OF THE SKY with power and great glory. And He will send forth His angels with A GREAT TRUMPET and THEY WILL GATHER TOGETHER His elect from the four winds, from one end of the sky to the other. (Matthew 24:29-31)

There will be *signs in sun and moon* and stars, and on the earth dismay among nations, in perplexity at the roaring of the sea and the waves, men fainting from fear and the expectation of the things which are coming upon the world; for the powers of the heavens will be shaken. Then they will see THE SON OF MAN COMING IN A CLOUD with power and great glory. But when these things begin to take place, straighten up and lift up your heads, because your redemption is drawing near. (Luke 21:25-28)

I WILL GRANT WONDERS IN THE SKY ABOVE AND SIGNS ON THE EARTH BELOW, BLOOD, AND FIRE, AND VAPOR OF SMOKE. THE SUN WILL BE TURNED INTO DARKNESS AND *THE MOON INTO BLOOD*, BEFORE THE GREAT AND GLORIOUS DAY OF THE LORD SHALL COME. (Acts 2:19-20)

I looked when He broke the sixth seal, and there was a great earthquake; and the sun became black as sackcloth made of hair, and *the whole moon became like blood*; and the stars of the sky fell to the earth,

as a fig tree casts its unripe figs when shaken by a
great wind. The sky was split apart like a scroll when
it is rolled up, and every mountain and island were
moved out of their places. (Revelation 6:12-14)

Putting all these passages together forms the biblical basis
for those who believe that something big is about to happen
in 2015. They believe that the references to signs in the sun
and the moon, the moon turning to blood, and the moon
not giving its light refer to lunar eclipses or blood moons,
especially the tetrad of blood moons in 2014–2015.

THE FOURTH TIME IS THE CHARM

The final clinching proof used to support the notion that
the four blood moons are a sign of some big change comes
from history. The blood moon tetrad in conjunction with
the Jewish feasts of Passover and Tabernacles has occurred
three times in the last five hundred years, and all three times
coincided with a major event involving the Jewish people
and/or the land of Israel. John Hagee highlights the rarity of
four blood moons falling on Jewish holidays:

A Tetrad is defined as four total lunar eclipses
(Blood Moons) that consecutively occur during
specific intervals of time. Lunar eclipses are relatively
common, but total lunar eclipses are less common.
A Tetrad is a rare occurrence and a Tetrad with

a total solar eclipse within its series is even rarer. Furthermore, a Tetrad linked to Jewish history has only happened three times in the past five hundred-plus years—it's very rare![7]

The first tetrad occurred in 1493–1494, one year after The Edict of Expulsion of the Jews was signed by King Ferdinand and Queen Isabella in Spain on March 30, 1492. The edict banned Jews from Spain if they failed to convert to Catholicism. The year before the tetrad of 1493–1494, Columbus sailed to the Americas, paving the way for the rise of the United States, which became a haven for the Jewish people from their perpetual persecution.

The second tetrad was in 1949–1950, one year after the founding of the modern state of Israel on May 14, 1948. The infant nation was attacked on every side by the surrounding Arab states (Egypt, Jordan, Iraq, Syria, Lebanon, and Saudi Arabia). The Jewish War of Independence spilled over into the early part of 1949. The Jewish people were victorious, and a truce was implemented, but settled peace still eludes Israel today.

The third tetrad transpired in 1967–1968. On June 5–10, 1967, Israel fought the famous "Six-Day War" against the combined forces of Egypt, Syria, and Jordan. The Jewish people turned a tragedy into a triumph, capturing the Sinai Peninsula from Egypt, the West Bank from Jordan, and the Golan Heights from Syria, and they seized control of Jerusalem.

In each of these three instances, the Jewish people faced struggle that was turned to success.

ISRAEL TIMELINE FROM 1948

1948 The state of Israel declares its independence and is attacked by six Arab nations.

1949 Jerusalem is divided into two parts (New City under Jewish rule; Old City under Jordanian rule).

1956 Israel, Great Britain, and France capture the Sinai from Egypt.

1964 The Palestinian Liberation Organization (PLO) is established.

1967 In the Six-Day War (June 5–10), Israel defeats Egypt, Syria, and Jordan and gains control of all Jerusalem, the Golan Heights, the West Bank of the Jordan River, and the Gaza Strip.

1973 On Yom Kippur (the Jewish Day of Atonement), Israel's holiest day, Egypt and Syria launch a surprise attack. After furious fighting, Israel turns them back.

1979 Israel and Egypt sign the Camp David Peace Agreement in which Israel agrees to return the Sinai Peninsula to Egypt in exchange for peace.

1982 Israel invades Lebanon in what was known as Operation Peace of Galilee.

1987–1993 The first *Intifada* (uprising) erupts in the West Bank and Gaza Strip.

1991 During the first Gulf War, Israel is hit repeatedly by Iraqi Scud missiles but does not retaliate.

1993 The Oslo Accords are signed. Israeli Prime Minister Yitzhak Rabin and PLO Chairman Yasser Arafat shake hands at the White House in the presence of President Bill Clinton.

2000 Israel withdraws from Lebanon. The second *Intifada* erupts in September when Ariel Sharon visits the Temple Mount.

2003 The "Quartet on the Middle East" (the United States, the European Union, Russia, and the United Nations) presents the "Road Map" for peace in the Middle East.
2005 Israel pulls out of all twenty-one settlements in the Gaza Strip.
2006 After terrorist incursions into Israel, during which soldiers are taken hostage, Israel wages a bloody thirty-four-day war with Hamas and Hezbollah.
2007–Present The Gaza conflict continues with intermittent talks of peace. Iran is enemy #1 for Israel as it presses toward the nuclear finish line.

Advocates of the blood moons prophecy contend that the historical precedent of the three previous tetrads and events involving Israel signals that something ominous will transpire in 2015 for Israel. John Hagee writes, "What were the common denominators of 1492, 1949, and 1967? They all centered on significant events related to Israel and the Jewish people, and they occurred on the Feasts of the Lord. . . . Each of the three previous series of Four Blood Moons began with a trail of tears and ended with triumph for the Jewish people."[8] But what about the fourth series? The question remains, is this really a reliable historical pattern? Will something significant happen again in Israel or possibly even in America in 2015?

THE FOURTH TETRAD

Three tetrads have come and gone. They're history. With all three, significant events happened around that time to the Jewish people and/or the land of Israel. One tetrad remains.

The unique alignment of science, history, and Scripture fuels speculation that something significant will occur for Israel and/or America in 2015. Moreover, the tetrad in 2014–2015 will be the last one in this century where blood moons fall upon Jewish feasts. Based on the convergence, John Hagee says, "This we know: things are about to change forever!"[9]

Or are they? Is there another way to look at the evidence? Does this view stand up to historical and biblical scrutiny? We will briefly examine each of the main arguments for the blood moons theory in the next several chapters, beginning with a look at the prophetic significance of Israel's feasts.

Chapter Five

SEVEN FEASTS AND FOUR BLOOD MOONS

. . . .

God gave Israel a calendar that was tied to the rhythm of the seasons and the history of the nation. It . . . anticipated what God would do for them in the future. . . . The future of the people of Israel [is] illustrated in these seven feasts.

—WARREN WIERSBE, *THE WIERSBE BIBLE COMMENTARY*[1]

MOST OF US keep a calendar. My wife keeps one at home that has all our social engagements, vacations, and other important activities written down. I have a calendar in my office that I use to plan out my entire year in advance. I write down all the conferences I attend, speaking opportunities, appointments, weddings I perform, other special events, and my preaching schedule. I use my calendar to keep things organized, to make sure I don't get overscheduled, and to stay on track to meet my goals and objectives. Not all my scheduled events for the year materialize, but keeping a calendar gives me an outline for what I hope to accomplish. I move through the year according to a planned timeline.

God also has a calendar, a program of scheduled events, and He is moving along that timeline with infallible precision. In His grace, God has given us that timeline in His Word so we can see where we are on it and so we can see that it's right on schedule. God has a plan for the entire world and all the nations, but He also has a special calendar for Israel, found in Leviticus 23, which describes the seven annual feasts. Warren Wiersbe calls Leviticus 23 "The Calendar That Tells the Future." Ray Stedman says this about God's calendar for Israel:

> His plan has not deviated by one hour or even one second. Events are never out of His control. Even though we do not always understand His schedule, God is in total, sovereign control of history. That is a great reassurance to us in perilous times. The twenty-third chapter of Leviticus is a remarkable portion of Scripture, because it gives us God's calendar for the appointed feasts of Israel. Those feasts were observed by the nation on a regular basis, year after year. There were seven feasts throughout the year, in addition to the weekly Sabbath. The feasts were precisely spaced and dated because they represented God's timetable of events by which He is moving through history.[2]

We need to understand the appointed feasts God gave Israel because the blood moons prophecy is linked to two of the feasts (Passover and the Feast of Tabernacles). During the blood moon tetrad in 2014–2015, each of the four blood moons will fall on a Jewish feast day. But we must also broach the topic of Israel's feasts because proponents of the blood moons prophecy claim that Israel's feasts have end-times significance for the church. In this chapter we'll get an overview of these feasts and how some of them relate to end-times events.

LIGHT FROM LEVITICUS

The book of Leviticus was the first book studied by Jewish children, yet it's often the last book of the Bible studied by most Christians.[3] Very few Christians spend much time in Leviticus, if any at all. During an annual schedule of reading through the Bible, this is where many believers bog down or even throw in the towel.

Leviticus 23 is a comprehensive catalog of the national annual feasts (or festivals) of Israel. It's one of those chapters you need to read completely in order to fully grasp its overall structure and message. I've included Leviticus 23 as an appendix in this book, so you can read it for yourself. I encourage you now to go to appendix 1 (pages 171–177) and read Leviticus 23. It's quite a chapter.

Now that you're back, let's make a few important observations about this chapter. First, the basic Hebrew word for "feast" is *hag*, which includes the idea of a pilgrimage and can be translated "pilgrim feast." Once the Jewish people entered the land of Israel and settled there, all male Israelites were required to make an annual pilgrimage to Jerusalem for three of the feasts: Passover, the Feast of Harvest (or Weeks, also known as Pentecost), and the Feast of Tabernacles (or Booths). Another Hebrew word, *moed*, is often translated "appointed times" or "appointed feasts." It carries the idea of "appointed meeting" or "set time" and occurs in the plural four times in Leviticus 23 (in verses 2, 4, 37, 44). There is debate about the exact number of annual feasts. Some see only six feasts—three in the spring and three in the fall—but I believe it's best to identify seven feasts, four in the spring and three in the fall.

The number seven is also prominent in Leviticus 23. Warren Wiersbe remarks, "The number seven is important in this calendar and in God's plan for Israel (Dan. 9:20-27). There are seven feasts, three of them in the seventh month. The Sabbath is the seventh day of the week. Pentecost is fifty days after firstfruits (seven times seven plus one). The Feast of Unleavened Bread and the Feast of Tabernacles each lasted seven days."[4]

The feasts are normally divided into two groups: the spring feasts and the fall feasts, which all occur in the seventh month on the Jewish lunar calendar, September–October on our solar calendar, every year. The spring feasts are Passover, Unleavened Bread, Firstfruits, and Pentecost. The fall feasts are Trumpets, the Day of Atonement, and Tabernacles.

THE FEASTS IN LEVITICUS 23		
Month	Modern Equivalent	Feasts
Nisan	March–April	Passover (*Pesach*)
Nisan	March–April	Unleavened Bread
Nisan	March–April	Firstfruits
Sivan	May–June	Weeks/Pentecost (*Shavuot*)

Tishri	September–October	Trumpets (*Rosh Hashanah*)
Tishri	September–October	Day of Atonement (*Yom Kippur*)
Tishri	September–October	Tabernacles/ Booths (*Sukkot*)

THE FOUR SPRING FEASTS

Passover

The spring feasts begin with Passover, which is observed on the fourteenth day of the first month on the Jewish calendar. Passover is the "foundation feast of the nation."[5] In the Exodus account of the first Passover night in Egypt, we read:

> Moses called for all the elders of Israel and said to them, "Go and take for yourselves lambs according to your families, and slay the Passover lamb. You shall take a bunch of hyssop and dip it in the blood which is in the basin, and apply some of the blood that is in the basin to the lintel and the two doorposts; and none of you shall go outside the door of his house until morning. For the LORD will pass through to smite the Egyptians; and when He sees the blood on the lintel and on the two doorposts, the LORD will pass over the door and will not allow the destroyer to come in to your houses to smite you." (Exodus 12:21-23)

God spared the firstborn from death in every house where the blood appeared around and above the door. From that point forward, the Jewish people celebrated Passover as a dramatic reminder of God's redemption of His people from Egyptian bondage through the blood of a lamb. As future generations ate the Passover, they commemorated God's salvation and passing over them in judgment. The ultimate fulfillment of Passover came at the cross of Jesus Christ. As 1 Corinthians 5:7 reminds us, "Christ, our Passover lamb, has been sacrificed" (NIV). That is the essence of the gospel: every person who trusts in Christ is safe from God's wrath under the blood of Christ.

Unleavened Bread

This second feast is closely linked to Passover. It begins the day after Passover and lasts for seven days. Like Passover, it looks back to Israel's time in Egypt, when God commanded the Israelites to remove all the leaven (yeast) from their houses. Just as yeast causes bread to rise, so sin causes our hearts to swell with pride. Jesus often likened sin to yeast or leaven (see Matthew 16:6; Luke 12:1). The Jewish people were reminded each year to remove all sin from their lives. In conjunction with Passover, the Feast of Unleavened Bread looks to the cross of Christ, where sin was put away.

Firstfruits

The third feast is called the Feast of Firstfruits. Every year before the spring harvest, on "the day after the Sabbath," the people took a sheaf of barley, cut it, and waved it before the Lord, offering Him the first and best of the harvest in recognition of His ownership of the land (Leviticus 23:11). Firstfruits marked the beginning of the barley harvest, the first grain of the year, and anticipated the full harvest to come.

We don't have to guess what the Feast of Firstfruits pictures. The New Testament tells us. Paul writes in 1 Corinthians 15:20-23, "Now Christ has been raised from the dead, *the first fruits* of those who are asleep. For since by a man came death, by a man also came the resurrection of the dead. For as in Adam all die, so also in Christ all will be made alive. But each in his own order: *Christ the first fruits*, after that those who are Christ's at His coming" (emphasis added).

When Jesus rose from the dead, He was the firstfruits of God's harvest. He rose on Sunday, the day after the Sabbath (Saturday), just as Leviticus 23:11 requires. His resurrection is the first installment or guarantee of more to follow. When He arose on Easter morning, He was the firstfruits of a great harvest of resurrected bodies to follow at the end of the age.

Weeks, or Pentecost

The fourth and final spring festival is given no name in Leviticus but is called the Feast of Weeks in Exodus 34:22. The Jewish people call it *Shavuot* or *Shabuoth*, which comes from the Hebrew word for "seven weeks." The children of Israel were told by God to count fifty days (seven weeks plus one day) from the Feast of Firstfruits and celebrate the Feast of Weeks. In English this feast is known as Pentecost, from the Greek word for "fifty." This feast was instituted to thank God for the wheat harvest. The firstfruits of the wheat harvest were presented to the Lord along with other offerings.

The Feast of Weeks typifies the coming of the Holy Spirit to bring Jews and Gentiles, represented by the two loaves of bread in Leviticus 23:17, "into one new man" on the Day of Pentecost (Ephesians 2:15; see Acts 2).

As you can see, a great event in history, associated with Christ's first coming, occurred on each of these spring feast days in the first century. Jesus died on Passover (April 3, AD 33).[6] Jesus was raised from the dead on Sunday, April 5, AD 33, which corresponded with the Feast of Firstfruits. Then, fifty days later at the Feast of Pentecost, the Holy Spirit came to baptize and indwell a group of Jewish people who were the initial members of the body of Christ, or the church. Each of the final great events of the earthly ministry of our Lord was fulfilled on the appointed day of the Jewish calendar. God keeps time with perfect precision.

THE SUMMERTIME OF HISTORY

After the four spring feasts, there is a long gap before the fall feasts begin in the seventh month. From mid-May, when Pentecost is observed, until the first day of the seventh month, there are no more feasts. The long summertime prophetically pictures the time between the first and second comings of

Christ—the present church age of almost two thousand years. Ray Stedman notes the significance of the long gap of time between the final spring feast and the first fall feast:

> The post-Pentecost age continues to this day. It has been many years since the day of the resurrection and since the day of Pentecost. We are in the summertime of human history, between the Feast of Pentecost and the next great feast, the next great moment in human history. For now, the door of the church is wide open to Jewish and non-Jewish people. In time, that door will be shut, but for now, all are welcome. This is where human history stands now.[7]

We're presently in the church age and may be on or very near the home stretch. The church age will end with the Rapture, and then God will take up His dealings again with the nation of Israel in the Tribulation and beyond, which is symbolized by the three fall feasts. God's long summer may be nearing its end. Based on the pattern with the spring feasts, one would conclude that significant prophetic events will line up with the dates of the fall feasts as well.

THE FALL FEASTS AND THE FUTURE

The final three feasts of Israel are celebrated in the seventh month on the Jewish calendar, the month of *Tishri*, which corresponds to our September–October.

Feast of Trumpets

Trumpets is a one-day celebration on the first day of the seventh month. It's a simple feast that included only blowing trumpets, offering special sacrifices, and abstaining from work. It signals the start of the Jewish New Year (the civil year), which today is called *Rosh Hashanah* ("head of the year").

The prophetic significance of the Feast of Trumpets is a debated issue. A growing group of people, including many proponents of the blood moons prophecy, believe that the Feast of Trumpets will be prophetically fulfilled at the Rapture. Some believe that while no one can know the *year* of Christ's coming, we can know the *day*—the Rapture will occur on the Feast of Trumpets.

The blowing of a trumpet ("the trumpet of God") is mentioned in conjunction with the Rapture in 1 Thessalonians 4:16. Also, 1 Corinthians 15:52 says, "in a moment, in the twinkling of an eye, at the last trumpet; for the trumpet will sound, and the dead will be raised imperishable, and we will be changed."

Arnold Fruchtenbaum, a Jewish believer in Christ and a prophecy expert, believes that the Rapture will fulfill the Feast of Trumpets:

> The "last trump" refers to the Feast of Trumpets and
> the Jewish practice of blowing trumpets at this feast
> each year. During the ceremony, there is a series of
> short trumpet blasts of various lengths, concluding
> with the longest blast of all, called the *tekiah gedolah*:

the great, or "last trump." Judaism connected this last trump with the resurrection of the dead, and so does Paul. Paul's point here is that the Rapture will be the fulfillment of the Feast of Trumpets.[8]

Fruchtenbaum, however, does not believe this means that the Rapture must occur on the specific day when the Feast of Trumpets falls. He notes that the death of Jesus also fulfilled the Day of Atonement, but that Jesus did not die on that day on the Jewish calendar. Therefore, he believes that the Rapture, while it will fulfill the Feast of Trumpets, does not have to occur on that specific day. This interpretation avoids the problems (discussed below) with setting a specific day for the Rapture.

There are two difficulties with relating the Feast of Trumpets with the Rapture. First, the feasts in Leviticus 23 are *Jewish* feasts. They're for the Jewish people, not the church. Of course, the church participates in the blessing of the death and resurrection of Christ, and Gentiles are blessed by the coming of the Spirit, but the basic interpretation of the feasts relates to Israel.

My view is that the Feast of Trumpets will find its fulfillment in the regathering of the Jewish people at the end of the Tribulation. This fits the Jewish nature of the feasts. Moreover, a trumpet will sound when the Jews are finally regathered to their land:

Immediately after the tribulation of those days THE SUN WILL BE DARKENED, AND THE MOON WILL NOT

GIVE ITS LIGHT, AND THE STARS WILL FALL from the sky, and the powers of the heavens will be shaken. And then the sign of the Son of Man will appear in the sky, and then all the tribes of the earth will mourn, and they will see the SON OF MAN COMING ON THE CLOUDS OF THE SKY with power and great glory. And *He will send forth His angels with A GREAT TRUMPET and THEY WILL GATHER TOGETHER His elect* from the four winds, from one end of the sky to the other. (Matthew 24:29-31, emphasis added)

The sounding of the trumpet at the end of the Tribulation to regather the scattered Jewish people, and not the Rapture, will fulfill the Feast of Trumpets. The "elect" are mentioned in Matthew 24:22, 24, and 31 and refer primarily to Jewish believers who survive the end-times tribulation. The entire context of Matthew 24 is Jewish, as there are references to the "holy place" in the Jewish Temple (24:15), people in "Judea" (24:16), and the "Sabbath" (24:20).

There's a second reason I don't believe the Rapture must occur on the Feast of Trumpets. To limit the Rapture to one day a year would destroy the doctrine of imminency, which means that Jesus could come at any moment. The New Testament presents the Rapture as an event that can happen at any time and that we should be constantly anticipating. These passages present a Rapture that is certain (though not necessarily soon), could happen at any moment, and could happen without warning:

- 1 Corinthians 1:7—"awaiting eagerly the revelation of our Lord Jesus Christ."
- Philippians 3:20—"Our citizenship is in heaven, from which also we eagerly wait for a Savior, the Lord Jesus Christ."
- Philippians 4:5—"The Lord is near."
- 1 Thessalonians 1:10—"to wait for His Son from heaven." (The word for "wait" in Greek is in the present tense, which means Christians are to wait continuously, and literally means to "wait up for," like parents waiting up for and looking for a child that they expect home at any moment.)
- Titus 2:13—"looking for the blessed hope and the appearing of the glory of our great God and Savior, Christ Jesus." (Why be constantly looking for Christ if He can't come at any moment?)
- Hebrews 9:28—"So Christ . . . will appear a second time for salvation without reference to sin, to those who eagerly await Him." (Why eagerly await His coming if it's a long way off?)
- 1 Peter 1:13—"Fix your hope completely on the grace to be brought to you at the revelation of Jesus Christ."
- Jude 1:21—"waiting anxiously for the mercy of our Lord Jesus Christ to eternal life."
- Revelation 3:11; 22:7, 12, 20—"I am coming quickly."
- Revelation 22:20—"He who testifies to these things says, 'Yes, I am coming quickly.' Amen. Come, Lord Jesus."

All these Scriptures refer to the Rapture and speak of it as though it could occur at any moment. There's nothing that is keeping it from happening. It will come without warning. If the Rapture can only occur on the Feast of Trumpets, then every year in the fall when that day passes, we would know that the Rapture couldn't happen for at least another year. There would be only one day a year when we could expect the Lord to come. If Christ can come only on one day, then He can't come any other day. The notion that Christ can come only on the Feast of Trumpets goes against the New Testament teaching of imminency. As Thomas Ice says,

> In spite of many recent trends to the contrary, date-setting is still prohibited in the Scriptures. Christ said, *"of that day and hour no one knows"* (Matt. 24:36). We may believe that we are near the general time of Christ's return since Israel is back in her land and other players are being placed on the end-time stage. However, Christ's rapture of His church is a signless event that could happen at any moment. When it does then God will complete His plan for Israel as forecasted in the three Fall Feasts of Israel. Meanwhile, the Feast of Trumpets does not in any way relate to the rapture of the church.[9]

The Day of Atonement

The sixth feast is the Day of Atonement, known as *Yom Kippur*. It is memorialized on the tenth day of the seventh month. Leviticus 16 provides a detailed description of sacrifices and duties of the Day of Atonement:

> "This shall be a permanent statute for you: in the
> seventh month, on the tenth day of the month,
> you shall humble your souls and not do any work,
> whether the native, or the alien who sojourns among
> you; for it is on this day that atonement shall be
> made for you to cleanse you; you will be clean from
> all your sins before the LORD. . . . Now you shall
> have this as a permanent statute, to make atonement
> for the sons of Israel for all their sins once every
> year." And just as the LORD had commanded Moses,
> so he did. (Leviticus 16:29-30, 34)

Yom Kippur was the only day every year when fasting was required and was the only day when the high priest could enter the Holy of Holies. Commentator R. Laird Harris explains, "People were to remain in their houses and remember that on this day their high priest was to enter the Most Holy Place bearing the name of their tribe on his breastpiece. . . . It was a proper and convenient time for repentance and spiritual preparation for the Feast of Tabernacles of the following week."[10]

The fulfillment of the Day of Atonement has several aspects. The death of Jesus paid the price once for all for sin. On the Day of Atonement the sins of the people were covered every year by the blood of a goat. To put it in our language today, the line of credit for sin was extended for another year. All the sins under the Old Covenant were put on credit and carried forward year after year. But at the Cross, Jesus didn't just cover sin for another year—He paid the full price for the permanent removal of sin. At the Cross, Jesus paid it all. Hebrews 9:11-12 says, "When Christ appeared as a high priest of the good things to come, He entered through the greater and more perfect tabernacle, not made with hands, that is to say, not of this creation; and not through the blood of goats and calves, but through His own blood, He entered the holy place once for all, having obtained eternal redemption." Lewis Sperry Chafer, who founded Dallas Theological Seminary, used to say, "Old Testament saints were saved on credit, but all the bills came due at Calvary."

The final fulfillment of the Day of Atonement is the national repentance and salvation of the Jewish remnant in the end times. Warren Wiersbe says it well: "After Israel is gathered to her land, the Jews will see their rejected Messiah, repent of their sins (Zech. 12:10—13:1), and be cleansed. The scattered nation will be gathered and the sinful nation will be cleansed. What a glorious day that will be!"[11]

Feast of Tabernacles

Whereas the Day of Atonement is a time of repentance and fasting, the Feast of Tabernacles, also known as the Feast of Booths (*Sukkot*) or Ingathering, is an occasion for great joy and thanksgiving. It is Israel's Thanksgiving Day. Like Passover and the Feast of Weeks, Tabernacles was a pilgrimage festival. All the men had to appear at the Tabernacle and later the Temple.

During this feast the people used branches to make booths (the Hebrew word for "booths" is *Sukkot*, which means "tent"). Commentator R. Laird Harris says, "The feast was a reminder of the Exodus from Egypt and the long trek to Sinai with the people living in tents. It would in future days be a reminder of the simple desert life when they walked with God as their head."[12]

Prophetically, the Feast of Tabernacles looks to the millennial reign of Christ and the rest of His people in their Promised Land. Warren Wiersbe writes, "The nation of Israel is not only a scattered people and a sinful people, but they're also a suffering people. No nation in history has suffered as the Jews have suffered, but one day their suffering will be turned into glory and joy. . . . For Israel, the best is yet to come! The scattered people will be gathered; the sinful people will be cleansed; the sorrowing people will rejoice."[13]

William MacDonald summarizes the feasts of the Lord and their relation to Israel's past, present, and future:

A definite chronological progression can be traced in the Feasts of Jehovah. The Sabbath takes us back to God's rest after creation. The Passover and the Feast of Unleavened Bread speak to us of Calvary. Next comes the Feast of Firstfruits, pointing to the resurrection of Christ. The Feast of Pentecost typifies the coming of the Holy Spirit. Then looking to the future, the Feast of Trumpets pictures the regathering of Israel. The Day of Atonement foreshadows the time when a remnant of Israel will repent and acknowledge Jesus as Messiah. Finally the Feast of Tabernacles sees Israel enjoying the millennial reign of Christ.[14]

THE PROPHETIC SIGNIFICANCE OF THE FEASTS	
The Feasts	*The Fulfillments*
Four Spring Feasts	**Christ's First Coming**
Passover and Unleavened Bread	The Cross
Feast of Firstfruits	The Resurrection
Feast of Weeks, or Pentecost	The Day of Pentecost
Summer	**The Current Church Age**
Three Fall Feasts	**Christ's Second Coming**
Feast of Trumpets	Israel's Regathering
Day of Atonement	Israel's Repentance
Feast of Tabernacles	Israel's Reign and Rest

FEASTS AND BLOOD MOONS

There's no doubt that the relationship between the blood moons and the Jewish feast days in 2014–2015 is intriguing. The blood moon tetrad in 2014–2015 is linked to Passover and the Feast of Tabernacles. The connection between the feasts and the four blood moons is the basis for the blood moons prophecy. But the critical question remains: Does this connection bear any prophetic significance for Israel or the world? Is it a harbinger of some big change in 2015? And even more important, does Scripture attach any significance to this linkage between the blood moons and the feasts?

In the next chapter, we'll examine the idea that God uses the heavens to speak to humanity and whether this adds support to the blood moons prophecy.

Chapter Six

MOONSHINE: SIGNS IN THE HEAVENS

The universe is but one vast symbol of God.

—THOMAS CARLYLE[1]

GOD'S CREATION DEFINITIVELY declares and displays His existence, creativity, power, and glory. As poet Gerard Manley Hopkins said, "The world is charged with the grandeur of God."[2] This idea comes from Scripture itself. Richard Swenson writes, "All throughout Scripture we read how God forged His creation and then indelibly stamped it with His glory."[3] Psalm 147:4 reminds us that God "counts the number of the stars; He gives names to all of them."

But perhaps Psalm 19:1-4 says it best:

The heavens are telling of the glory of God;
And their expanse is declaring the work of His hands.
Day to day pours forth speech,
And night to night reveals knowledge.
There is no speech, nor are there words;
Their voice is not heard.
Their line has gone out through all the earth,
And their utterances to the end of the world.

The heavens display God's glory, but according to Scripture, at special times they also serve as signs of coming events. The foundation of the blood moons prophecy is that God uses the heavens to signal His intentions to humanity on earth—that the heavens are God's "billboard." The beginning point for this belief is Genesis 1:14: "God said, 'Let there be lights in the expanse of the heavens to separate the day from the night, and let them be for signs and for seasons and for days and years.'"

John Hagee says, "The Hebrew word for 'sign' is *owth*, which also translates as 'signals.' Therefore, based on the Bible, God uses the sun, moon, and stars as *signals* to mankind. He uses the heavens as His divine billboard announcing coming events. What is God trying to say to us?"[4] Jack Kelley analyzes the use of Genesis 1:14 by proponents of the blood moons prophecy:

> To make the passage read more easily in English, the [King James Version's] translators inserted the word "and" in several places in this verse. . . . Inserting the additional articles makes the King James version look like the lights are for signs as well as to mark the seasons, days and years. But I think the interlinear [a more literal rendering] is closer to the original intent of Genesis 1:14. The NIV translation agrees. It reads, *Let there be lights in the expanse of the sky to separate the day from the night, and let them serve as signs to mark seasons and days and years.* All this to

say it's not clear that Genesis 1:14 says one of the functions of the lights in the sky is to serve as signs of important events.[5]

I agree. I believe that reading Genesis 1:14 as implying that God uses the heavens as "high-definition billboards" to send messages to humanity is overstating what the verse says.

Having said that, I do believe Scripture declares that signs will appear in the heavens in the future time of global tribulation and especially in conjunction with the second coming of Jesus to earth. Jesus said as much in Luke 21:25-26: "There will be signs in sun and moon and stars, and on the earth dismay among nations, in perplexity at the roaring of the sea and the waves, men fainting from fear and the expectation of the things which are coming upon the world; for the powers of the heavens will be shaken."

The vast majority of Bible prophecy teachers agree that God uses cosmic signs as precursors of end-times events. The question is what kinds of heavenly signs does God use, and when will Luke 21:25 be fulfilled? (We'll examine this and other Scripture passages in detail in the next chapter.)

LUNAR LOCAL

Another key problem related to the four blood moons as God's "high-definition billboard" is that much of the world won't even see them, especially the part of the world they're supposed to impact. How can something be a global sign that "something is about to change" or a "divine billboard announcing coming events," as Hagee asserts, if most people in the world are unaware of it? Dr. Danny Faulkner of Answers in Genesis highlights this serious shortcoming with the blood moons prophecy:

> There also is a question of from what portion of the earth one ought to view these eclipses for them to constitute a sign. One might think that Jerusalem would be a key site, but the first three total lunar eclipses in 2014–2015 won't be visible from there, and only the beginning of the final eclipse will be. . . .
>
> The first eclipse (March 20, 2015) is total. Having personally experienced one total solar eclipse, I can testify that a total solar eclipse is stunning and awe-inspiring. . . . But how many people will witness this particular eclipse? The eclipse path is in the North Atlantic and Arctic Oceans. The only landfalls that the eclipse path will make are the Faroe Islands and Svalbard. . . . The eclipse is of short duration, and the weather can be overcast much of the time at that latitude. There is a good chance that few people, if any, will actually see this eclipse.

Faulkner concludes, "Not actually witnessing these events but instead just knowing that somewhere some sort of solar eclipses are happening seems to fall far short of being specific and spectacular signs of end times."[6]

Concerning the first blood moon on April 15, 2014, NASA reports, "None of the eclipse is visible from north/east Europe, eastern Africa, the Middle East or Central Asia."[7] Notice that the Middle East will totally miss the first blood moon of 2014. The same is true of the second blood moon on October 8, 2014.[8]

Jack Kelley points out that of the previous series of lunar tetrads, "only the one in April 1950 was fully visible from Israel, four others were partially visible and the rest were not visible at all. (Since these are being touted as signs to Israel, you might wonder why they weren't all visible there.)"[9]

In contrast to the lunar tetrad of 2014–2015, the cosmic portents in Scripture will be visible and unmistakable to everyone around the globe (see Matthew 24:29-30; Revelation 1:7; 6:12-16). When Jesus returns to earth, His coming will be dramatically heralded by cosmic signs. The limited visibility of the blood moons works against the idea that they are a sign of some dramatic change. Moreover, proponents of the blood moons prophecy maintain that the first lunar tetrad that fell on the Jewish feasts of Passover and Tabernacles occurred in 1493–1494, before modern means of communication. I wonder if people at that time in the parts of the world where the blood moons weren't visible had any idea they were even happening. Today, with global communication, we know things that happen all over the world, but such was not the case in 1493–1494. Something can't be a sign if you never see or know about it. Those who maintain that the four blood moons are a portent that something is about to change need to explain how something hidden to most of the world, and especially to those in Israel, can serve as a dramatic sign of the times for them. This is a serious problem.

THE BETHLEHEM STAR

Supporters of the blood moons prophecy point to the Bethlehem star at the first coming of Christ as a biblical example of signs in the heavens signaling that something big is about to happen on earth. When the Magi (wise men) arrived in Jerusalem, they said, "Where is He who has been born King of the Jews? For we saw His star in the east and have come to worship Him" (Matthew 2:2). Then, after they were informed by the Bible scholars of that day that the Messiah would be born in Bethlehem, the wise men redirected their journey there. Matthew 2:9-10 continues the story: "After hearing the king, they went their way; and the star, which they had seen in the east, went on before them until it came and stood over the place where the Child was. When they saw the star, they rejoiced exceedingly with great joy."

As you can imagine, there are many views concerning the nature of the star that led the Magi from their home in the East all the way to Jerusalem and ultimately to the very house where Jesus was living. Here are some of the suggestions.

- Halley's comet passed overhead in 12 BC—but this is too early, since Christ was probably born in about 4 or 5 BC.
- Johannes Kepler held that the conjunction of the planets Saturn and Jupiter in 7 BC in the zodiacal sign of Pisces would have shined brightly and that Pisces was connected in ancient astrology with the Hebrews. This, too, seems too early to fit the chronology of Christ's birth.
- A supernova.

Many other planetary conjunctions have similarly been suggested.[10] The word *star* (*aster* in Greek) can be used figuratively to represent a great brilliance, shining, or radiance. Jesus refers to Himself figuratively as "the bright morning star" (Revelation 22:16). The view I hold is that the "star" that appeared was not a heavenly body or natural phenomenon, but a supernatural shining created by God to guide the wise men to the Savior. R. C. Sproul supports this view:

> The other possibility is that the star that led these men to Jerusalem and then to Bethlehem was a specific creation by God for this particular event, something like the shekinah glory cloud that led the people of Israel in their wilderness wandering. . . . I think it would be very difficult to follow the tail of a comet, or even an inordinately bright conjunction of two planets, to Jerusalem and then from Jerusalem

to Bethlehem. I suspect that this is another account
of a miraculous work of God to guide the men to the
proper place.[11]

Whatever the star was, it led the wise men to the very
house where Jesus was living with his parents (see Matthew
2:9). No literal star in the distant heavens could provide such
precise guidance. John MacArthur notes, "The Shekinah
glory of God stood over Bethlehem just as, centuries before,
it had stood over the Tabernacle in the wilderness. And just
as the pillar of cloud gave light to Israel but darkness to Egypt
(Ex. 14:20), only the eyes of the magi were opened to see
God's great light over Bethlehem."[12]

Dramatic cosmic events were associated with Christ's birth
and His death. But, again, I believe the "star" that appeared
over Bethlehem was a supernatural event, not a natural event
like a lunar eclipse. Likewise, the darkness that enveloped
Calvary for the final three hours of Christ's suffering on the
cross was supernatural. The Bible never tells us how far the
three hours of darkness extended from Calvary. The darkness
may have been limited to the area around Calvary, or it may
have extended to the entire city of Jerusalem or even to all
of Israel, and possibly to the entire globe. We simply don't
know for sure, but whatever its scope, there was no natural
explanation. In the same way, the cosmic signs that portend
Christ's return will also be supernatural phenomena. (We'll
look at this in more depth in the next chapter.)

Some might argue that the Bethlehem star—like the

blood moons—was limited in its visibility to only the wise men, just as the blood moons will be visible only to some part of the world. But we have to remember that the appearance of the star to the wise men was not *intended* as a global sign. The star was a special sign to guide the wise men to the house where Jesus was staying so they could worship Him, whereas the signs that point to the Lord's Second Coming are intended to be global.

CONCLUSION

God uses the heavens at critical junctures to signal the coming of great events. He will use them in the end times to portend the second advent of Christ. But the four blood moons of 2014–2015 fail as a discernible sign of the times for the simple reason that they will not be visible to most of the world, and most specifically, not to Israel, which is supposed to be the focal point of the blood moons prophecy.

For these reasons, the first key prong of the blood moons prophecy is without merit. Let's turn now to the specific biblical passages that refer to blood moons and examine their relationship, if any, to the lunar tetrad.

Chapter Seven

BLOOD MOONS AND BIBLE PROPHECY

I looked when He broke the sixth seal, and there was a great earthquake; and the sun became black as sackcloth made of hair, and the whole moon became like blood.

—REVELATION 6:12

BLOOD MOONS PROPHECY proponents maintain that science, history, and the Bible have aligned in an unprecedented convergence that points undeniably to the significance of the four blood moons as omens of coming events. As we have seen, science confirms the blood moon tetrad in 2014–2015, and some believe that history reveals that when three previous tetrads occurred, the Jewish people experienced momentous events (we'll discuss the historical angle in the next chapter). But the central question remains: Does the Bible predict the occurrence of blood moons in conjunction with the end times? Do ancient biblical prophecies reveal that the four blood moons are an omen of coming catastrophe? This is the most important issue concerning blood moons because the Word of God is our final guide on the future—thus, it's our final word on the blood moons prophecy.

Before looking at the individual passages that mention the moon turning to blood, I want to establish a basic framework for biblical interpretation. When searching for the meaning of any biblical text, a literal, normal approach to the text is essential. In his book *The Interpretation of Prophecy*, Paul Lee Tan defines this approach: "Literal interpretation of the Bible simply means to explain the original sense of the Bible according to the normal and customary usages of its language."[1] In other words, with a literal approach, we do not expand meaning beyond what the words themselves say and customarily mean. How is this done? It can only be accomplished through the *grammatical* (according to the rules of grammar), *historical* (consistent with the historical setting of the passage), *contextual* (in accordance with its context) method of interpretation. All of these elements are essential to sound biblical interpretation, but especially important is context. The context of a passage sets the limits of what that text can mean. Those who are advocating the blood moons prophecy are, in my opinion, guilty of flawed interpretation. I believe they often fail to account for chronological indicators in the surrounding context, read meaning that is not there into numerous texts, and in other cases fail to account for all the elements that are present in the particular passage.

Let's briefly examine each of the five main biblical passages that refer to signs in the moon or in the heavens in reference to the end times, paying special attention to the immediate context and what each text says and does not say.

JOEL 2

The prophecy of Joel was written to the disobedient people of Israel, calling them to repentance. Joel prophesied the "day of the Lord" in his own time, which was a scorched-earth locust plague, sent by God to discipline His rebellious people (see Joel 1:15). The Old Testament refers to the "day of the Lord" nineteen specific times (see Isaiah 2:12; 13:6, 9; Ezekiel 13:5; 30:3; Joel 1:15; 2:1, 11, 31; 3:14; Amos 5:18 [2 times]; 5:20; Obadiah 1:15; Zephaniah 1:7, 14 [2 times]; Zechariah 14:1; Malachi 4:5). The New Testament mentions the "day of the Lord" four times (see Acts 2:20; 1 Thessalonians 5:2; 2 Thessalonians 2:2; 2 Peter 3:10). From these passages, we learn that the Day of the Lord is anytime that God dramatically, directly intervenes in history, usually in judgment but sometimes in blessing. There have been numerous historical Days of the Lord. For example, the destruction of Egypt by the Babylonians under King Nebuchadnezzar was called the "day of the Lord" in Ezekiel 30:1-4.

The locust plague in Joel was a Day of the Lord when God intervened directly to judge Israel (see Joel 1:15). Yet it is important to remember that all past, historical days of the Lord prefigure the final, future Day of the Lord. The army of locusts invading Israel in Joel's day foreshadowed the final human army that will invade Israel during the campaign of Armageddon at the end of the Tribulation.

Joel 2:30-31 appears in the midst of his sobering prophecy and is the biblical beginning for the specific teaching on blood moons:

I will display wonders in the sky and on the earth,
Blood, fire and columns of smoke.

The sun will be turned into darkness
And the moon into blood
Before the great and awesome day of the LORD comes.

According to these verses there will be cosmic convulsion in conjunction with the coming Day of the Lord in the end times. The created order will react to the glorious presence of the Lord. Two other times in the prophecy of Joel we find references to the moon growing dark as an ominous sign of impending judgment. The first is in Joel 2:10:

Before them the earth quakes,
The heavens tremble,
The sun and the moon grow dark
And the stars lose their brightness.

The locust plague described in Joel 2 serves as a graphic precursor of the final Day of the Lord and the literal armies God will bring against Israel at the campaign of Armageddon.

The other reference in Joel to the moon growing dark is in Joel 3:15. The surrounding context of this verse again indicates this is the final campaign of Armageddon, when the armies of the earth gather against Israel:

Hasten and come, all you surrounding nations,
And gather yourselves there.
Bring down, O LORD, Your mighty ones.
Let the nations be aroused

And come up to the valley of Jehoshaphat,
For there I will sit to judge
All the surrounding nations.
Put in the sickle, for the harvest is ripe.
Come, tread, for the wine press is full;
The vats overflow, for their wickedness is great.
Multitudes, multitudes in the valley of decision!
For the day of the LORD is near in the valley of
    decision.
The sun and moon grow dark
And the stars lose their brightness.
The LORD roars from Zion
And utters His voice from Jerusalem,
And the heavens and the earth tremble.
    (Joel 3:11-16, emphasis added)

The context indicates that both Joel 2:10 and Joel 3:15 refer to the moon growing dark in connection with the final Day of the Lord and the events of Armageddon. Consider also Revelation 14:14-19 with its allusions to Joel 3:13:

Then I looked, and behold, a white cloud, and sitting on the cloud was one like a son of man, having a golden crown on His head and a sharp sickle in His hand. And another angel came out of the temple, crying out with a loud voice to Him who sat on the cloud, "Put in your sickle and reap, for the hour to reap has come, because the harvest of the earth is ripe." Then He who sat on the cloud swung His sickle over the earth, and the earth was reaped.

And another angel came out of the temple which is in heaven, and he also had a sharp sickle. Then another angel, the one who has power over fire, came out from the altar; and he called with a loud voice to him who had the sharp sickle, saying, "Put in your sharp sickle and gather the clusters from the vine of the earth, because her grapes are ripe." So the angel swung his sickle to the earth and gathered the clusters from the vine of the earth, and threw them into the great wine press of the wrath of God.

The allusions to Joel 3:13 in Revelation 14:14-19 confirm the view that Joel is referring to Armageddon in his prophecy.

Three things about Joel 2:30-31 are important to correctly interpret its meaning and timing. First, whenever the moon is turned to blood, Joel 2 says that other things will happen at the same time. Notice that the biblical prophecies about the moon turning to blood also involve solar and stellar phenomena, as well as wonders on earth. Hagee points out that there will be a total solar eclipse on March 20, 2015, in conjunction with the four blood moons happening in 2014–2015. He points to this as a fulfillment of verses that mention the sun being darkened. While that is debatable, when in 2014–2015 will there be "blood, fire and columns of smoke"? We have to consider *all* of this prophecy in order for it to be fulfilled, not just selected parts of it. Selective interpretation can lead to all kinds of problems.

Second, I believe the "great and awesome day of the LORD" is not the same as the "day of the LORD." The future Day of the Lord is an extended period of time when God will intervene dramatically, first in judgment (the seven-year Tribulation) and then in blessing (the thousand-year reign of Christ on the earth). The Day of the Lord will commence with the beginning of the Tribulation. The first phase of the Day of the Lord will be a time of unparalleled judgment on the earth.

The Joel 2:30-31 passage distinguishes the "day of the LORD" from the "great and awesome day of the LORD." I believe the latter is the actual day of Christ's second advent, the particular day of Christ's return to earth. The great and awesome Day of the Lord is *the* day when Jesus comes. If I'm correct about this, then the setting for the sun being darkened and the moon turning to blood will be just before the second advent of Christ, which cannot be in 2014–2015 since we aren't in the seven-year Tribulation that must precede it. (See chapter 3, where I discuss the "end-times script" of events that must take place before the Tribulation, the most obvious of which is the Rapture of believers to heaven followed by the rise of the final world leader and his brokering of a peace treaty with Israel.) So I don't believe Joel 2 supports the blood moons prophecy.

MATTHEW 24

Jesus talked a lot about the future. In fact, He may have talked about the future more than any person who ever lived. It's clear from His many discussions, debates, and discourses that He wants His followers to know what's coming in the end times. In His great prophetic sermon in Matthew 24–25, Jesus gives the basic blueprint or outline of the events that will immediately precede His coming. Matthew 24–25 is the greatest prophecy sermon ever preached. It is most often called the "Olivet Discourse" because Jesus preached the sermon on the east side of the Mount of Olives, which overlooks the Temple area in Jerusalem, but it's also dubbed the "Mini Apocalypse" because it provides a concise yet comprehensive overview of the end times. Some call it the "Eschatological Discourse" because it previews the end of the age or "The Prophetic Discourse" since it prophesies the future.

Jesus gave this sermon or discourse in response to a question from His disciples about the destruction of the Temple and the end of the age. Matthew tells us that before arriving at the Mount of Olives, Jesus and His disciples had been in Jerusalem on the Temple grounds. As they left, Jesus made a monumental statement: "Do you not see all these things? Truly I say to you, not one stone here will be left upon another, which will not be torn down" (Matthew 24:2). As Jesus and the disciples made their way across the Kidron Valley to the Mount of Olives, these words must have been seared into the minds of the disciples. They must have wondered how this could be. When would this happen? When would the end come?

When Jesus and His disciples finally arrived at the Mount of Olives, four of His disciples—Peter, James, John, and Andrew—came to Him for some further clarification: "When will these things happen, and what will be the sign of Your coming, and of the end of the age?" (Matthew 24:3). There is some debate about how many questions the disciples asked Jesus. Many (including John Hagee) divide it into three separate questions:

1. When will these things be? (When will the Temple be destroyed, as Jesus had stated in Matthew 24:2?)
2. What will be the sign of Your coming?
3. What will be the sign of the end of the age?

While it is possible that the disciples had two or three questions in mind, it is best to see that in the minds of the disciples, they were thinking of one big question with three parts. Clearly, the disciples' question focuses on the return of Christ and the end of the world. For the disciples, the destruction of the Temple, the coming of the Messiah, and the end of the world all comprised one great complex of events (see Zechariah 14:1-11).[2] The sermon by Jesus covers the second coming of Christ and the time immediately preceding His coming, or what is commonly called the time of tribulation. That will be the time when the birth pangs begin that signal the end of the age.

Imagine what it must have been like to hear the Savior outline the blueprint of the end times in such an intimate setting. This sermon of Jesus sketches a checklist of the signs of the times. Jesus' sermon is a *Reader's Digest* condensed version of the book of Revelation. Jesus told us many things in His great discourse from the Mount of Olives, but one point comes through loud and clear: this world is not going to become a better place to live in. Times of almost unbelievable difficulty are on the horizon. Jesus said that the end of the age will be a totally unique time of terror. Nothing in all of world history will even compare to what is coming. It will totally eclipse all previous history in terms of hardship and trouble. Jesus made it crystal clear: "There will be a great tribulation, such as has not occurred since the beginning of the world until now, nor ever will" (Matthew 24:21).

Jesus follows a chronological outline in unfolding the key events of the end of the age. He uses four main phrases that highlight landmarks or signposts of the end times.

"The Beginning of Birth Pangs"

Jesus answered and said to them, "See to it that no one misleads you. For many will come in My name, saying, 'I am the Christ,' and will mislead many. You will be hearing of wars and rumors of wars.

See that you are not frightened, for those things must take place, but that is not yet the end. For nation will rise against nation, and kingdom against kingdom, and in various places there will be famines and earthquakes. But all these things are merely the beginning of birth pangs." (Matthew 24:4-8)

This refers to the first three and a half years of the coming seven-year Tribulation period. The beginning of the birth pangs is outlined in Matthew 24:4-14. The close parallels between Matthew 24 and Revelation show that both passages are describing the same future time.

PARALLELS BETWEEN MATTHEW 24:4-14 AND REVELATION 6-7	
Matthew 24	Revelation 6-7
False Christs (24:4-5)	Rider on the White Horse (6:1-2)
Wars and Rumors of Wars (24:6-7)	Rider on the Red Horse (6:3-4)
Famines and Earthquakes (24:7)	Rider on the Black Horse (6:5-6)
Famines and Plagues (24:7; Luke 21:11)	Rider on the Pale Horse (6:7-8)
Persecution and Martyrdom (24:9-10)	Martyrs (6:9-11)
Terrors and Great Cosmic Signs (Luke 21:11)	Terror (6:12-17)
Worldwide Preaching of the Gospel (24:14)	Ministry of the 144,000 (7:1-8)

"The Abomination of Desolation"

> Therefore when you see the ABOMINATION OF
> DESOLATION which was spoken of through Daniel
> the prophet, standing in the holy place (let the
> reader understand), then those who are in Judea
> must flee to the mountains. Whoever is on the
> housetop must not go down to get the things out
> that are in his house. Whoever is in the field must
> not turn back to get his cloak. But woe to those who
> are pregnant and to those who are nursing babies in
> those days! But pray that your flight will not be in
> the winter, or on a Sabbath. (Matthew 24:15-20)

The setting up of the abomination of desolation refers
to the Antichrist defiling the rebuilt Temple in Jerusalem,
first by sitting in the Holy of Holies and declaring that he
is God, and then by making an image of himself that all the
world will be required to worship (see 2 Thessalonians 2:4;
Revelation 13:14-15). This decisive event will occur at the
midpoint of the Tribulation.

"Great Tribulation"

> There will be a great tribulation, such as has not
> occurred since the beginning of the world until now,
> nor ever will. (Matthew 24:21)

Jesus' reference to "great tribulation" is the final half of the Tribulation period that will immediately precede His Second Coming.

"But Immediately after the Tribulation of Those Days"

But immediately after the tribulation of those days
THE SUN WILL BE DARKENED, AND THE MOON WILL
NOT GIVE ITS LIGHT, AND THE STARS WILL FALL
from the sky, and the powers of the heavens will
be shaken. And then the sign of the Son of Man
will appear in the sky, and then all the tribes of the
earth will mourn, and they will see the SON OF MAN
COMING ON THE CLOUDS OF THE SKY with power and
great glory. And He will send forth His angels with
A GREAT TRUMPET and THEY WILL GATHER TOGETHER
His elect from the four winds, from one end of the
sky to the other. (Matthew 24:29-31)

Beginning in Matthew 24:29, Christ's second coming is unveiled. Notice it will happen "immediately after the tribulation of those days." The litany of signs enumerated by Jesus in Matthew 24 culminates with verses 29-31.

According to John Hagee, "The Bible clearly describes both blood moons and a solar eclipse in Joel 2:30-31 and Acts 2:19-20, and Jesus confirms them in Matthew 24:29."[3]

There are several problems with using Matthew 24:29 to support the blood moons prophecy related to 2014–2015.

First, Matthew 24:29 appears to say that the sun being darkened and the moon not giving its light will happen at the same time. This makes sense since the moon merely reflects the light of the sun—if the sun is darkened, the moon won't give its light. If this view is correct, then this cannot refer to the blood moons in 2014–2015. None of these blood moons will occur at the same time as the darkening of the sun or a solar eclipse. A solar eclipse will occur on March 20, 2015, but this will not happen at the same time as any of the four blood moons.

Second, I believe the sun being darkened and the moon not giving its light in Matthew 24:29 is a supernatural occurrence, not a predictable solar and lunar eclipse. God will darken the sun and the moon as a supernatural sign of His Son's return (see Revelation 16:10-11). Just as supernatural darkness blanketed the world (or at least Jerusalem) for the final three hours during the time of Jesus' death, in the same way God will smother the world in darkness during the Tribulation. The same sign of darkness was used by God during the Egyptian plagues. God brought darkness over the land of Egypt for three days, but the Israelites had light in their homes (see Exodus 10:22-23). These were supernatural signs of God's judgment.

Third, and most significantly, notice the timing of these heavenly signs. They occur "immediately after the tribulation of those days" (Matthew 24:29). These signs occur at the *end* of the coming seven-year time of Tribulation. The years 2014–2015 cannot be the time frame this passage is talking about because, as noted above, we are not yet in the

Tribulation. The entire seven-year Tribulation period must occur before Christ can return to earth in glory. The blood moons prophecy of 2014–2015 cannot be the fulfillment of Matthew 24:29.

Fourth, Matthew 24:29 says that at the same time the sun is darkened and the moon does not give its light, "THE STARS WILL FALL from the sky, and the powers of the heavens will be shaken." Those who hold to the four blood moons prophecy never explain clearly, that I'm aware of, how the stars falling and the shaking of the heavens relate to 2014–2015. Commentator Leon Morris says, "The most striking thing is that neither *the sun* nor *the moon* will give any light; the whole earth will lie in darkness. With that is joined disturbance in *the stars*, for they *will fall from heaven*. . . . That the stars will fall means that starlight is affected as much as is sunlight and moonlight. There is to be no source of light here on earth in that day."[4] The detailed terms of this prophecy do not fit the four blood moons that will occur in 2014–2015; rather, they preclude it.

LUKE 21

Two days before He died on the cross, Jesus said,

> There will be signs in sun and moon and stars, and
> on the earth dismay among nations, in perplexity at
> the roaring of the sea and the waves, men fainting
> from fear and the expectation of the things which

are coming upon the world; for the powers of the heavens will be shaken. Then they will see THE SON OF MAN COMING IN A CLOUD with power and great glory. But when these things begin to take place, straighten up and lift up your heads, because your redemption is drawing near. (Luke 21:25-28)

I agree that there will be cosmic signs in conjunction with the glorious return of Jesus to earth. Jesus clearly said so. But again, we have to keep the context before us. In this passage, Jesus is referencing His second advent to earth. Just as there was a sign in the heavens at His birth (the star the wise men followed—see my discussion in chapter 6), and deep darkness over the earth at His death, there will be heavenly signs attending His return. Yet the blood moons in 2014–2015 cannot be the signs Jesus is referring to in Luke 21:25. The heavenly portents Jesus predicted will happen at the end of the time of Tribulation as immediate precursors of Christ's return. Once again, since the time of Tribulation has not started yet, and it will last for seven years, nothing in 2014–2015 can be the fulfillment of Jesus' prophecy. The blood moon tetrad of 2014–2015, while interesting, cannot fulfill these words of Jesus.

ACTS 2

The fourth passage used to support the blood moons prophecy is from Acts 2, which quotes the Joel 2 passage we looked at earlier. Acts 2 is a record of Peter's great sermon in the

Temple precincts in Jerusalem on the Day of Pentecost—the first sermon of the church age. The Spirit had come in power to indwell Peter and the others gathered in the upper room and to baptize them into the newly formed body of Christ. As an outward sign of this inward work, the apostles spoke in various languages (tongues) that they had never learned, "speaking of the mighty deeds of God" (Acts 2:11).

Some in the gathered crowd began to ask, "What does this mean?" while others accused Peter and the apostles of hitting an early happy hour (see Acts 2:12-13). In response to the questions and accusations, Peter preached a powerful sermon. He opened the discourse with a lengthy quote of Joel 2:28-32, which includes the words, "I will grant wonders in the sky above and signs on the earth below, blood, and fire, and vapor of smoke. The sun will be turned into darkness and the moon into blood, before the great and glorious day of the Lord shall come" (Acts 2:19-20). The same issues I brought up earlier that apply to Joel 2 and the blood moons apply to Peter's quote from Joel in Acts 2. The settings of both Joel 2 and Acts 2 have nothing to do with 2015. While Peter quoted these verses to show that the last days had arrived with the coming of the Spirit, nothing even remotely similar to the signs in Acts 2:19-20 happened on the Day of Pentecost. In AD 33, when the Spirit came, there was no literal "blood, and fire, and vapor of smoke." If we take the moon turning to blood literally, then we have to take these other signs literally as well, and nothing like that happened on the Day of Pentecost. The mention of the "last days" in Acts 2 refers to the time that began with the descent of the Spirit and extends all the way to Christ's second coming (see Hebrews 1:2). This current age is even called the "last hour" elsewhere in Scripture (see 1 John 2:18). The final fulfillment of Joel 2 awaits the repentance of the Jewish people and Christ's return.

REVELATION 6

Revelation 6:1 begins the breaking of the seven seals on the scroll that the Father gives to Jesus in Revelation 5:1-8. The only document in that day that was sealed with seven seals was a will. The seven-sealed scroll in Revelation 6 is the Father's will to the Son. The inheritance is the Kingdom. Revelation 6–16 chronicles the opening of this scroll and the series of judgments it brings.

When the scroll is completely unrolled, Jesus Christ receives His full inheritance—the kingdoms of this world (see Revelation 11:15). Christ's rule over the world and His full inheritance will be realized when He comes again (see Revelation 19) and establishes His kingdom on earth (see Revelation 20:1-6).

The first four seals are often called the "four horsemen of the apocalypse"—the white, red, black, and pale horses and their riders. I like to call them "riders on the storm" because each horse and rider brings a storm of judgment to the earth. The fifth seal is martyred believers in heaven during the Tribulation who cry out to God for vindication.

The sixth seal is described in Revelation 6:12-14:

I looked when He broke the sixth seal, and there
was a great earthquake; and the sun became black as
sackcloth made of hair, and the whole moon became
like blood; and the stars of the sky fell to the earth,
as a fig tree casts its unripe figs when shaken by a
great wind. The sky was split apart like a scroll when
it is rolled up, and every mountain and island were
moved out of their places.

There are two main problems with relating this verse to the
blood moons of 2014–2015. First, the context of Revelation
6:12-14 is during the future seven-year Tribulation on earth.
My view is that the sixth seal is opened at about the midpoint of the Tribulation (see chart on page 43), but whether
or not you agree with that, if you believe this happens some
time into the seven-year Tribulation, then this cannot be
related to blood moons in 2014–2015 for the simple reason that, as discussed earlier in this chapter, we are not in
the Tribulation yet. Connecting the blood moons in 2014–
2015 to Revelation 6 would require us to already be in the
seven-year Tribulation of the end times, which we are not.
The context of Revelation 6 eliminates the blood moons of
2014–2015 from constituting its fulfillment.

Second, notice the full content of Revelation 6:12-14.
The moon becoming like blood is just one of *six* cosmic signs
that will occur. The other five are:

- A great earthquake (in Greek, a *megas seismos*)
- The sun becoming as sackcloth made of hair
- The stars of the sky falling to the earth (It will appear
  from humanity's perspective that the stars are falling.
  This probably refers at the very least to extremely
  large meteor showers. From the vantage point of
  earth, heavenly bodies will look like they are dropping
  like figs from a tree.)
- The sky splitting apart like a scroll
- The mountains and islands moving

While the sun becoming like sackcloth could refer to a solar eclipse that will occur on March 20, 2015, in the middle of the four blood moons, when will the rest of these signs occur? Proponents of the blood moons position ignore these other signs that will accompany the moon becoming like blood. Consistency demands that all of these signs must be present for Revelation 6:12-14 to be literally fulfilled. For these reasons, I believe the *context* and *content* of Revelation 6:12-14 have no relation to the blood moon tetrad of 2014–2015.

MISSING MOONS AND MOONSHINE

Having examined the five passages used to support the blood moons prophecy, I think the strongest biblical evidence against this alleged prophecy is something I've not yet mentioned: that the Bible never specifically mentions *four* blood moons. Don't miss this pivotal point. None of the verses quoted to support this theory mention *four* blood moons. The entire blood moons prophecy is based on something the Bible never specifically predicts. The Bible *does* mention the moon turning to blood in connection with Christ's return, but it never mentions *four* blood moons, let alone four blood moons in conjunction with the Jewish feasts of Passover and Tabernacles. What the Bible *does not* say about the four blood moons is critical. The silence is very significant when it comes to assigning meaning to this phenomenon. Building a view that contends something major is about to change in our world on something the Bible never actually predicts is shaky at best and irresponsible speculation at worst.

Let me reiterate that I do believe in signs of the end times. I believe there are legitimate signs today that point toward the coming of Christ, and I have no personal ax to grind against the blood moons prophecy or its proponents. Nevertheless, I think a fair, contextual reading of the five biblical passages used to support this view shows its sizable shortcomings.

But aside from the biblical issues with this position, there are more problems with its view of history.

Chapter Eight

ONCE IN A BLOOD MOON

• •

The sun, the moon, and all the ethereal host

Seem'd as extinct: day ravish'd from their eyes,

And all heaven's splendours blotted from the skies.

—HOMER, *THE ILIAD*

MARK BILTZ of El Shaddai Ministries, who pioneered much of the blood moons prophecy, says,

> The last time there were four blood moons in a row . . . falling on the feast days was in 1967 and 1968 when Israel recaptured Jerusalem. The time before that was the two years right after they became a nation in 1948. You can't help but stand there with your mouth opened wide with the impeccable timing and signals sent to the world by the Creator of the universe.[1]

There's no doubt that each time the lunar tetrad occurred in the past, significant events transpired around the same time for the Jewish people and/or the land of Israel. But is the evidence as straightforward as the prophecy's proponents would lead us to believe? Before we get ahead of ourselves, let's consider each of the past tetrads to understand how the blood moons related to the events they purportedly signified.[2]

THE FIRST TETRAD: FOUR BLOOD MOONS OF 1493–1494

The Spanish Inquisition

04/02/1493 . . . . Passover

09/24/1493 . . . . Total Solar Eclipse

09/25/1493 . . . . Feast of Tabernacles

03/22/1494 . . . . Passover

09/15/1494. . . . . Feast of Tabernacles

COLUMBUS DAY: THE BLOOD MOONS OF 1493–1494

In 1492, the Great Expulsion occurred when Jews who refused to convert to Catholicism were permanently banished from Spain. King Ferdinand and Queen Isabella signed the Edict of Expulsion on March 30, 1492. The edict is chilling to read. It is anti-Semitism on full display. Here is the pertinent part of the edict that commanded all Jews to leave Spain:

> Therefore, we . . . resolve to order the said Jews
> and Jewesses of our kingdoms to depart and never
> to return or come back to them or to any of them.
> And concerning this we command this our charter
> to be given, by which we order all Jews and Jewesses
> of whatever age they may be, who live, reside, and

exist in our said kingdoms and lordships, as much
those who are natives as those who are not, who by
whatever manner or whatever cause have come to live
and reside therein, that by the end of the month of
July next of the present year, they depart from all of
these our said realms and lordships, along with their
sons and daughters, menservants and maidservants,
Jewish familiars, those who are great as well as the
lesser folk, of whatever age they may be, and they
shall not dare to return to those places . . . under pain
that if they do not perform and comply with this
command . . . they incur the penalty of death and the
confiscation of all their possessions by our Chamber
of Finance, incurring these penalties by the act itself,
without further trial, sentence, or declaration.[3]

As every American knows, 1492 was the same year that
Columbus sailed to the New World, funded in part by
money confiscated from the Jews. America became a haven
for the Jews from oppression. In keeping with the promise
to Abraham in Genesis 12:1-3, God has abundantly blessed
America for its favorable treatment of the Jewish people over
the centuries, and we should all pray that it will continue.

Concerning the blood moon tetrad in 1493–1494, John
Hagee says, "The expulsion of the Jews from Spain in 1492
was a world-changing moment. The mantle of prosperity was
lifted from Spain and placed upon the shoulders of an infant
nation that would become the United States of America.

God Almighty used the Four Blood Moons of 1493–94 as a *heavenly billboard* to mankind."[4]

While it is true that the expulsion of the Jews from Spain was an important occurrence in Israel's history, I see several problems with Hagee's statement. First, the four blood moons of 1493–1494 occurred *after* the expulsion of the Jews from Spain in 1492 and the discovery of the New World. Since the blood moons appeared after the fact, how did they serve as a *sign* of the event? Something can't be a sign of a coming occurrence if it happens after the event. By definition, a sign must occur before the event it signals. Consider, for instance, if you are driving down the highway and see a sign for an exit after you pass it. That sign isn't much help. In the same way, the blood moon tetrad of 1493–1494 cannot be a sign of what happened a year or two earlier in 1492. This just doesn't fit the definition of a sign. The four blood moons should have occurred in 1490–1491 or even 1491–1492 to be a sign of an event in 1492.

Another difficulty with the blood moons theory, which I've already mentioned, is that lunar eclipses are not visible worldwide. And depending on weather conditions, the visibility may be inhibited even where they could be seen. If the coming blood moons are signs of God's dealings with Israel and the world, they have to be visible to effectively serve that purpose. This problem was even greater in 1493–1494, before the advent of modern technology and global communication.

Today, with NASA and other astronomy experts and with global means of communication, the general public knows about total lunar eclipses even if we can't see them. But the same was not always true in the past, certainly not in 1493–1494, at the time of this tetrad. If these blood moons are God's high-definition billboard of His dealings with man, then what about the people who can't witness the event? Or don't see it due to poor visibility? Or never know it occurred? Something can only serve as a discernible sign if people can see it or at least know about it. That was not the case for most of the world in 1493–1494.

Moreover, in a day when communication was severely limited, how many people in the world were even aware of the Edict of Expulsion in Spain in 1492? Most people in the world knew nothing about the Great Expulsion of the Jews or the discovery of the New World. And, as noted previously, lunar eclipses are not global events. So, it's worth asking—how can the blood moon tetrad of 1493–1494 be a sign of an event in 1492 that most of the world at the time never saw and never knew occurred?

THE SECOND TETRAD:
FOUR BLOOD MOONS OF 1949–1950

Israel's Struggle for Survival and Independence

04/13/1949	Passover
10/07/1949	Feast of Tabernacles
04/02/1950	Passover
09/12/1950	Total Solar Eclipse
09/26/1950	Feast of Tabernacles

INDEPENDENCE DAY:
THE BLOOD MOONS OF 1949–1950

As early as 1871, for the first time since AD 135, the Jewish people began to return to their ancient homeland. About twenty-five thousand Jews had settled there by 1881. Theodor Herzl, who assembled and led the First Zionist Congress in 1897 in Basel, Switzerland, became known as the father of modern Zionism. At the congress, the following statement was officially adopted: "Zionism seeks to establish a home for the Jewish people in Palestine secured under public law." The Zionist Congress and its actions marked a watershed in the modern history of the Jewish people. Nevertheless, in spite of Herzl's heroic efforts, the number of Jews in the land had only climbed to eighty thousand by 1914.

Another major turning point in the history of modern Israel occurred near the end of World War I, when Arthur J. Balfour, the British Foreign Secretary, issued what has become known as the Balfour Declaration on November 2, 1917. The now-famous declaration was included in a personal letter from Balfour to Lord Rothschild, a wealthy Jewish entrepreneur. In the letter, Secretary Balfour gave approval to the Jewish goal of return and repossession of their Promised Land. The declaration simply said, "His Majesty's Government views with favor the establishment in Palestine of a national home for the Jewish people."

Unfortunately for the Jewish people, Arab opposition to any notion of Jewish reclamation of their ancient homeland derailed any further pursuit or enactment of the Balfour Declaration. However, the hope expressed in the declaration served as a stimulus for more Jews to return to the land, and by the outbreak of World War II in 1939, about 450,000 Jews had managed to return to the Middle East.

The 1930s and 40s were the darkest hour for the Jewish people as they languished and suffered systematic extermination in Nazi death camps. Any faint hope for a national homeland was dashed. The chief concern of European Jews was simply survival. Nevertheless, in what could only be explained as a twist of providential irony, Hitler's heinous atrocities provided the greatest momentum for the establishment of a national homeland for the Jews. The worldwide outpouring of sympathy for their plight paved the way for the United Nations' approval of the formation of the nation of Israel, which transpired on May 14, 1948. The new nation received five thousand square miles of territory, which supported a population of 650,000 Jews and several hundred thousand Arabs.

But Israel's rebirth was not without serious complications. Israel was simultaneously attacked on all sides by Egypt, Jordan, Iraq, Syria, Lebanon, and Saudi Arabia, threatening its very existence. Israel's War of Independence lasted until 1949, but the ongoing conflict with its neighbors still continues today.

The birth of the modern state of Israel in May 1948 was definitely a prophetic game changer. No event since the death and resurrection of Christ and the coming of the Spirit at Pentecost has been viewed as more important to God's prophetic plan. The rebirth of Israel is the supersign of the end times. Almost every other end-times prophecy hinges in one way or another on the presence of the Jewish people in their land. But the blood moon tetrad of 1949–1950 suffers from the same basic problem as the previous one: the blood moons of 1949–1950 happened after the fact. Israel's rebirth occurred on May 14, 1948, so the lunar tetrad of 1949–1950 cannot serve as a sign for it. Supporters of the blood moons prophecy will contend that Israel's War for Independence did indeed continue on into the early part of 1949, but all would agree that the main event was May 14, 1948, which occurred before the four blood moons. Something cannot be considered a sign if it postdates what it's supposed to signify.

THE THIRD TETRAD: BLOOD MOONS OF 1967–1968

The Six-Day War

04/24/1967 . . . . Passover

10/18/1967 . . . . . Feast of Tabernacles

11/02/1967 . . . . . Total Solar Eclipse

04/13/1968. . . . . Passover

10/06/1968. . . . . Feast of Tabernacles

JERUSALEM DAY: THE BLOOD MOONS OF 1967–1968

After the War of Independence in 1948–1949, Israel fought the Suez War in 1956 against Egypt and its leader, Gamal

Abdel Nasser, when he nationalized the Suez Canal. On October 29, 1956, Israel invaded the Sinai Peninsula and took control but later returned the Sinai to Egypt.

Then, on June 5, 1967, the Six-Day War erupted. Israel's victory was overwhelming. The Jewish state captured the Sinai Peninsula from Egypt, the West Bank from Jordan, and the Golan Heights from Syria, and seized control of Jerusalem.

In the case of this third tetrad, a major event in Israel did happen after the blood moon tetrad began. Israel's Six-Day War, on June 5–10, 1967, happened after the first blood moon appeared but before the final three.

JUDGMENT DAY?: THE BLOOD MOONS OF 2014–2015

What do these historical blood moon tetrads mean for 2014–2015? If we follow the historical pattern of the lunar tetrads in 1493–1494 and 1949–1950, then we should have expected a monumental event in Israel the year *before* the blood moons began to appear, which would have been 2013. Or if we follow the pattern in 1967–1968, some great event should occur between the first and second blood moons, that is, mid-2014. My point is simple: the historical evidence for the blood moons prophecy is not as airtight or compelling as some might claim. The dates for the tetrads do not consistently align, or align in the same way, with the events they supposedly signify, and the total lunar eclipses were either not known about, not seen, or both.

When people initially hear about the first three tetrads and their proximity to major events in Israel's history, it appears very impressive. Yet upon closer examination, the strength of the evidence withers. Make no mistake—the blood moons prophecy makes serious claims. Its proponents maintain that something big is about to happen to Israel and to the United States if we fail to repent. But using historical precedent that is close but not exact to prove an important point is sloppy and gives unwarranted weight and credibility to the blood moons prophecy.

Chapter Nine

THE DATING GAME

· ·

As a Christian I take it for granted that human history will some day end; and I am offering Omniscience no advice as to the best date for that consummation.

—C. S. LEWIS, "IS PROGRESS POSSIBLE?"[1]

THE DETAILS OF Christ's return have been the subject of much speculation throughout America's history, but speculation was especially prevalent in the American Northeast of the early 1800s. Several factors—including the financial panic of 1839—gave rise to the belief that Christ's return was imminent. In fact, people were so concerned about the end of the world that newspapers ran notes about prophecies side-by-side with news about current events and stock listings.

William Miller was one of the chief speculators. He predicted in 1818 that Christ would return between March 21, 1843, and March 21, 1844. His predictions flavored his sermons, and because of his charisma and confidence, he drew a large crowd of supporters and his teachings spread rapidly across New England. Some took him so seriously that they sold their possessions and gave up their livelihoods. When March 21, 1844, passed without event, the prediction was altered to October 22, 1844.

Despite the earlier failed prediction, people still gathered together on October 22 to witness the end of the world. When nothing happened, many Christians lost interest or faith. Unbelievers scoffed. The aftermath of these failed predictions was fewer conversions and the end of a fruitful period of revival. The event is remembered today as the "Great Disappointment."[2] Miller's movement led to the founding of the Seventh-Day Adventists.

Long before the Great Disappointment and many times since, people have set dates for the coming of the Lord or other end-times events. Unfortunately, date setting has a long history. There seems to be something within many people that can't avoid the temptation to speculate about the timing of future events.

DOOMSDAY DATE SETTERS

To illustrate the frequency and folly of date setting, follow along as I recount a few of the more recent, notable examples of those who have predicted Christ's coming or the end of the world.

1914: Jehovah's Witnesses founder Charles Taze Russell set 1874 as the date of Christ's return. After that, their leaders continually earmarked various years: 1878, 1881, 1910, 1914, 1918, 1925, 1975, and 1984. After nine wrong dates, they claim to have given up on predicting the time of Christ's coming.

1988: Edgar C. Whisenant, a former NASA engineer, wrote *On Borrowed Time* and *88 Reasons Why the Rapture Will Be in 1988*, predicting that Christ would return between September 11 and 13, 1988, on the date of that year's Rosh Hashanah or the Feast of Tabernacles. Whisenant is quoted as confidently saying, "Only if the Bible is in error am I wrong; and I say that to every preacher in town."[3] He also boldly asserted, "If there were a king in this country and I could gamble with my life, I would stake my life on Rosh Hashanah [19]88."[4] When his Rapture prediction failed, Whisenant followed up with books predicting various dates in 1989, 1993, and 1994. None of those books sold very well.

1994: Harold Camping, in his book *1994?*, predicted the Lord's return on September 6, 1994. The book was packed with numerology that added up to 1994 as the date of Christ's return.

1997: The appearance of the Hale-Bopp Comet in 1997 sparked a terrible tragedy when thirty-nine members of the Heaven's Gate, an American UFO doomsday cult based in San Diego, California, committed mass suicide in order to join what they believed was an alien spacecraft following the comet, which was then at its brightest.

2000: Based on a connection between the six days of Creation, God's rest on the seventh day, and 2 Peter 3:8, a few of the early church fathers taught that the earth would last only six thousand years. Second Peter 3:8 says, "With the Lord one day is like a thousand years, and a thousand years like one day." Since God rested on the seventh day, they believed the final thousand years of history would be a Sabbath rest for the earth or the thousand-year reign of Christ (the Millennium). This mistaken interpretation was seized upon, and it added to the Y2K hysteria for January 1, 2000, even generating some predictions of the end of the age around the turn of the century.

2008: On the basis of certain feast days and blood moons, some predicted the Rapture would occur in September 2008. I spoke at a prophecy conference not long before September 2008, where this view was presented, and I talked with the speaker about his predictions. He assured me that he wasn't saying "for sure" that Jesus would come, but he did everything but set a date.

2011: Undeterred by his previous miscalculation in 1994, Harold Camping gave the "dating game" another try when he predicted the end of the world on May 21, 2011. When that date passed uneventfully, Camping made one final prediction that the Lord would come on October 21, 2011. After that false prophecy failed, a chastened Camping admitted he was wrong and pledged to make no further predictions. He died in 2013.

The list of date setters and doomsday predictors could go on and on, but you get the point—date setters are batting .000. They are "O-fer." Whenever someone sets a date for any end-times event, Armageddon, or the coming of Jesus Christ, I like to say that you can be sure that's not the day. Jesus said as much in Matthew 24:42, 44: "Be on the alert, for you do not know which day your Lord is coming. . . . For this reason you also must be ready; for the Son of Man is coming at an hour when you do not think He will" (see also Matthew 25:13; Acts 1:7).

In spite of the unambiguous teaching of Jesus and the pitiful track record of those who have tried to predict the date for future events related to the end times, people persist in setting dates. What's startling is that Jesus claimed that during His earthly ministry even He did not know the day of His coming. He said, "Of that day and hour no one knows, not even the angels of heaven, nor the Son, but the Father alone" (Matthew 24:36). Claiming to know the specific time of Christ's coming is claiming to know something that the Father didn't reveal even to His Son during His earthly ministry. This is the apex of arrogance and foolishness.

To be fair to proponents of the blood moons prophecy, most of them have avoided setting a specific date for the Lord's coming, which the Bible strictly forbids. This point must not be overlooked or misstated. Nevertheless, they are naming a specific year when a major event will occur related to the end times. They consistently mark the year 2014–2015 as a time when something big will happen. Some have even said specifically that if America doesn't repent, something cataclysmic will hit the United States in 2015. I consider this to be a milder form of date setting, but date setting nonetheless. They have set 2014–2015 as a date when a prophetically significant event will occur.

The serious biblical problem with this approach is that God's Word nowhere, and especially not in the book of Revelation, singles out a specific year or even a decade or century when we can pinpoint some specific event. Every Christian should avoid date setting of any kind because Jesus forbade it, and when the predicted event doesn't occur, it gives the Bible a black eye. Every date that is set and then passes without fulfillment heightens unbelievers' (and believers') skepticism and scoffing, even toward legitimate biblical prophecy. I believe the blood moons prophecy falls within, or at least perilously close to, the date-setting danger zone, and for this reason should be rejected.

SHEMITTAH YEARS AND 2015

In support of the prediction that something big is about to happen in 2015, John Hagee notes that 2015 will be a Shemittah or Sabbatical year and that something significant has happened in every Shemittah year in the past that God uses to capture the world's undivided attention. Remember that a Sabbatical year was every seventh year, when the Jewish people were to allow their fields to rest (see Leviticus 25).

To prove the prophetic significance of these Sabbatical

years, Hagee points out the Shemittah years from 1973, as well as some key event that occurred that year:

- 1973—The *Roe v. Wade* decision by the US Supreme Court
- 1980—Saddam Hussein's invasion of Iran and the beginning of the Gulf Wars
- 1987—A supernova visible without a telescope for the first time since 1604; the US stock market's drop
- 1994—Yasser Arafat's return to the Middle East; an earthquake along the New Madrid fault line in the United States
- 2001—The 9/11 terrorist attack against the United States
- 2008—The US stock market crash and a 777-point decline of the Dow Jones on one day (September 29), "the greatest one-day decline in the history of Wall Street"[5]

Adding seven years to 2008 brings us to 2015, when, Hagee says, something big will happen that will change everything. Hagee does not say what the event will be, but he leaves little doubt that it will be something significant. The Shemittah year begins on September 25, 2014, and ends on September 13, 2015, both dates aligning with the Jewish Feast of Trumpets. Hagee warns, "The final Four Blood Moons are signaling that something big is coming . . . something that will change the world forever."[6]

I have two main issues with this line of reasoning. My first and biggest disagreement is that the Jewish Sabbatical year applied to the people and land of Israel under the old covenant. America, along with all other nations, is not under the Mosaic law and is not required to keep either the Sabbath day every week or the Sabbatical year every seven years. Applying the Sabbatical year from the Mosaic law to America is contrary to all normal, sound methods of biblical interpretation.

My second problem with this line of thinking is that for it to be true, one would have to continue going back every seven years from 1973 all the way back to the first century, when the church of Jesus Christ came into being, to really prove this theory. Why begin arbitrarily with 1973? If we go back seven years before 1973, what happened in 1966 that was of such earth-shattering significance? Or seven years before that in 1959? (Well, I was born in 1959, but I don't think that qualifies, although my mother might disagree.)

Another issue is that almost every year something happens that one could point to as a significant event that captures the world's attention. In our increasingly uncertain, volatile world, troubles are mushrooming. The year 2015 will probably be no different. Something big could happen in Israel or somewhere else on earth in 2014 or 2015. I'm not denying that. I don't know the future. With all the problems and dangers in the world today, especially in Israel, it's not far-fetched to envision something big happening in Israel at any time. The lid on the Middle East could blow off at any moment. With Iran poised to cross the nuclear finish line and the chaos in Syria and Egypt, almost anything seems possible. Blood moons prophecy advocates will undoubtedly find something in 2014–2015 that they can point to as a fulfillment arising from the appearance of the four blood moons. In that case, the prophecy becomes self-validating, but also meaningless.

It may be easy to find some event in 2015, no matter how unspectacular, to make this a self-validating prophecy. But whatever occurs, it won't be the second coming of Christ to earth and won't be related to the blood moons of 2014–2015. I don't want to appear overly cynical, but I believe blood moons prophecy advocates will find something in 2015 to point to as the fulfillment of the alleged prophecy. But even this won't substantiate the blood moons prophecy since it is not based on sound biblical interpretation, which is where we must begin and end all discussions of prophecy.

FOCUS ON THE FIG TREE

Many proponents of the blood moons prophecy appeal to another New Testament passage to bolster their view and narrow down the time of Christ's coming. Matthew 24:32-34 says,

> Learn the parable from the fig tree: when its branch
> has already become tender and puts forth its leaves,
> you know that summer is near; so, you too, when
> you see all these things, recognize that He is near,

right at the door. Truly I say to you, this generation will not pass away until all these things take place.

Many, including John Hagee, believe that the picture of the fig tree is a reference to the nation of Israel since this image was used to represent Israel in the Old Testament.[7] They say that the budding of the fig tree referenced in Matthew 24:32 occurred in May 1948, and the generation that sees Israel reborn will be the generation that sees Christ's return. Based on this passage, Hagee believes we are *that* generation.[8]

Since a generation is normally forty to sixty years, some expected Christ to come by 1988 or 2008. The year 1988 became a common time to set a date for the coming of the Lord, as we saw earlier in this chapter. Sadly, some prophecy preachers fell into this trap. When Christ didn't return in 1988, the length of a generation was extended to sixty years and then to eighty years, or the date of the fig tree's budding was changed to June 1967, when the Jews took the city of Jerusalem. That extends the "generation" out perhaps as far as 2027, depending on how long a generation can be stretched. John Hagee sets the time for a generation at one hundred years, meaning that Christ must come by 2048.[9] This constant changing of the length of a generation is further evidence of the folly of setting specific dates or even time frames for end-times events.

Beyond the evidence of the shifting date, I don't think this time frame is necessary because I don't believe the fig tree in Matthew 24 has anything to do with the rebirth of the nation of Israel. John MacArthur says, "A popular version of that view is that the budding of the fig tree refers to Israel's becoming a political state in 1948. Because Jesus does not identify the fig tree as Israel, that meaning would have been totally obscured to the disciples and to every other believer who lived before the twentieth century."[10] John Walvoord and Charles Dyer add:

> Actually, while the fig tree could be an apt illustration of Israel, it is not so used in the Bible. In Jeremiah 24:1-8, good and bad figs illustrate Israel in the captivity, and there is also mention of figs in 29:17. The reference to the fig tree in Judges 9:10-11 is obviously not Israel. Neither Matthew 21:18-20, nor Mark 11:12-14 with its interpretation in 11:20-26, give any indication that this is referring to Israel, any more than the mountain referred to in the passage. Accordingly, while this interpretation is held by many, there is no clear scriptural warrant for doing so.[11]

I believe that Matthew 24:32-34 means that the generation which personally witnesses the signs in Matthew 24:4-30—that is, the Tribulation period—will not pass away before Christ returns. Thus, this verse should not be used to establish a specific time frame or cutoff point for the coming of Christ. Jesus is merely using a natural illustration that anyone could understand. He is saying that just as one can tell summer is near by the blossoming of the fig tree, so those alive in the Tribulation will be able to see that His coming is near when the signs predicted in Matthew 24:4-31 begin to happen. The words "all these things" in Matthew 24:33 refer to all the signs in the preceding context. Walvoord and Dyer note, "The signs in this passage, accordingly, are not the revival of Israel, but the tribulation itself. . . . That Israel's presence in the Holy Land is a dramatic evidence that the age is approaching its end may be supported by other passages, but this is not the point here."[12]

The thrust of prophecy in Scripture is that we are to live as if Jesus could come at any moment. That's all we can do. We must leave the timing of this event with the Lord. All I can legitimately say when people ask me how close we are to the end is that I sincerely believe that Jesus could come today, and I pray that He will. That's the only date we should ever set for the Lord's coming—He may come today!

IN HIS TIME

The reason the Lord didn't tell us when He's coming or when any other end-times event is scheduled is simple: God wants His people to be ready all the time. Think about it. If we knew the date of any specific event related to the end times, we would be tempted to be indifferent and apathetic if it was in the distant future and panicked and hysterical if it was near. By hiding the timing of future events from humanity, God calls us to always stand ready (see Matthew 24:42–25:13).

So, can we know *when* the end times will arrive? No! Can we know the time, even the year of any future event? Not a chance. Can we know the day of the Rapture? I don't believe so. We should stay far away from any semblance of date setting whatsoever, not even get close to it. No one should set any year, month, or day for any future event. Date setting is futile and foolish. Date setters are upsetters, fostering unnecessary worry and in some cases even hysteria and panic. No one knows when any end-times event will occur except God, and He hasn't identified any specific year or day. This reinforces the wise saying that "the purpose of Bible prophecy is not for us to make a calendar, but to build character."[13]

We must always remember that God's timetable is not our timetable. The apostle Peter prophesied that scoffers will come in the last days questioning the promise of Christ's return (see 2 Peter 2:1-4). Part of Peter's answer to these mocking skeptics is to inform them that God's view of time is very different from ours. Peter reminds us that "with the Lord a day is like a thousand years, and a thousand years are like a day" (2 Peter 3:8, NIV). God's timetable is not our timetable.

But one thing we can know for sure is that Christ's coming is closer than ever. I like the familiar story of the man who was sitting downstairs late one night reading while his wife had already retired to bed. He heard the grandfather clock begin to chime in the hallway and started counting the chimes to see what time it was. The clock chimed nine, ten, eleven, twelve, then thirteen. Upon hearing the thirteenth bell, he got up, ran up the stairs, bolted in to wake his wife, and said, "Honey, wake up—it's later than it's ever been!" That's the one answer we can safely give when people want to know what time it is. We are closer to the Lord's coming than we've ever been. However, we still must confess that no one knows for sure how close we are to the end except the Lord.

J. Gregory Sheryl reminds us of the proper perspective as we await our Lord's coming.

> One thing believers can know with certainty is that Christ's return is closer every day. . . . Knowing that Christ may return at any moment, believers say with Paul, "O Lord, come!" (1 Cor. 16:22). And the Bible ends with the same prayer: "And the Spirit and bride say, 'Come!' And let the one who hears say, 'Come!' And let him who thirsts come. And whoever desires, let him take the water of life freely. . . . He who testifies to these things says, 'Surely I am coming quickly.' Amen. Even so, come, Lord Jesus" (Rev. 22:17, 20).[14]

I do believe that there are signs indicating that Christ's coming could be very near, but we still must confess that we don't know the specific day, the hour, or the year of His coming or of any other prophetic event. We can confidently say, "Jesus may come today," but must also humbly admit that He may not come in the next decade. He may not come even in my lifetime or in yours. God's timetable is not ours, but we can be sure that someday God's promise will be fulfilled.

Prophecy teacher Ed Hindson says it well: "God's clock, the clock of history, is ticking away. It never speeds up and never slows down. It just keeps on ticking, continually and relentlessly, moving us closer and closer to the end of the age. How close we are to the end will only be revealed by time itself. Don't gamble with your eternal destiny. Time may very well be running out."[15] We can be sure that someday it will. Make sure you are ready when it does.

Chapter Ten

BLOOD MOONS
AND YOU

. . . .

If our global Titanic is nearing a cosmic iceberg, personally I
want to know. If the world system is rushing toward collapse,
truth matters. If the time for sipping tea on the veranda is
over, then let's move on to the things that matter most.

—RICHARD A. SWENSON, *HURTLING TOWARD OBLIVION*[1]

THE CURTAIN FOR the final drama of the ages may be ready to go up, not because of the appearance of the four blood moons, but because there are other clear signs of the times. There will undoubtedly be many unexpected twists and turns as the clock of time ticks down to earth's final hour, but it's only a matter of time until the world is shocked by the Rapture and plunged into the coming time of tribulation. As that time approaches and as the blood moons prophecy continues to attract more and more attention, we need to keep our hope fixed on Jesus Christ and make sure we are living in light of His coming.

Dr. John Walvoord highlights the practical effect of Christ's any-moment return on our daily lives: "The hope of the Lord's return should constitute an impelling challenge. The task is large and the days are few. It is time for searching of heart and purification of life. It is time for prayer and devotion, for sacrifice and effort. Now is the time to preach the good news of a Savior who died for the sins of the whole world that all who believe might live. . . .The coming of the Lord is as near as your next breath, the next beat of our hearts, the next word of our lips."[2]

I've argued throughout this book that the blood moons prophecy does not stand up to scrutiny—biblical or otherwise. My final word of exhortation is this: don't get caught up or carried away in any speculation about some great cataclysmic event in 2015 surrounding the appearance of the blood moons. Instead, follow the practical, biblical guidelines for living in light of the end that are given in 1 Peter 4:7-11:

> The end of all things is near; therefore, be of sound judgment and sober spirit for the purpose of prayer. Above all, keep fervent in your love for one another, because love covers a multitude of sins. Be hospitable to one another without complaint. As each one has received a special gift, employ it in serving one another as good stewards of the manifold grace of God. Whoever speaks, is to do so as one who is speaking the utterances of God; whoever serves is to do so as one who is serving by the strength which God supplies; so that in all things God may be glorified through Jesus Christ, to whom belongs the glory and dominion forever and ever. Amen.

First Peter 4:7-11 tells us that as we await the Lord's coming, we need to do four things: keep our heads clear, our hearts warm, our homes open, and our hands busy.

It's true that the Rapture *could* happen in 2014 or 2015. It can happen any time. Nothing must happen before Jesus can return to rapture His people to heaven. The Rapture is a signless, any-moment event, so it could happen in 2015 or any day before that time or after it. The Rapture is an imminent event. The trumpet can sound at any time. We are called to always be looking for the coming of Christ, not on some specific day, but every day. Not at some specific time, but all the time. The most important question is—are you ready?

Once, in a reply to a delegation of bank presidents who considered whether it was time to give up all thought of the Union, President Abraham Lincoln told the following story:

> When I was a young man in Illinois . . . I boarded
> for a time with a deacon of the Presbyterian Church.
> One night I was aroused from my sleep by a rap at
> my door, and I heard the deacon's voice exclaiming,
> "Arise, Abraham, the day of judgment has come!"
> I sprang from my bed, and rushed to the window;
> and saw the stars falling in a shower. But I looked
> beyond those falling stars, and far back in the
> heavens I saw—fixed, apparently, and immovable—
> the grand old constellations with which I was so
> well acquainted, fixed and true in their places. No,
> gentlemen, the world did not come to an end then,
> nor will the Union now![3]

As Abraham Lincoln wisely observed, fixed points of reference help us keep our bearings in a world that is constantly turning and churning. Many, like the old deacon, are sounding the alarm that something dramatic will happen in 2014–2015, maybe even the Lord's coming. In times like these, we need some fixed reference points, some immovable anchor points to steady our faith and calm our nerves. Here are some truths we can put our trust in.

THE SOVEREIGNTY OF GOD

Our first anchor point in times like these is the sovereignty of God. I like the story of the man who went to visit his psychic, but when he arrived, there was a sign on the office door that read, "Closed Due to Unforeseen Circumstances." Thankfully, there are no unforeseen circumstances with God. There's never panic in heaven. The Trinity never has to meet in emergency session.

The main prophetic name of God in the book of Revelation is "Almighty." The Greek word is *Pantokrator*, which appears nine times in the book of Revelation and literally means to "hold everything in your hands" or to "have your hands on everything." God is Sovereign. He is Almighty. He has His hands on everything. The words to the old song really are true—"He's got the whole world in His hands." There's no need to be afraid of the future if you have trusted in the Lord. God has it all under control. As someone has aptly said, "History is *His-story*." That includes your past, your present, and your future. Bible prophecy finds its origin in a Sovereign God who revealed it to us not to scare us but to prepare us. Not to make us anxious but to make us aware.

I had the privilege of attending the Fiesta Bowl with my family in January 2012 to watch our alma mater, the Oklahoma State University Cowboys, play the Stanford Cardinals. Oklahoma State fell behind early 14–0 but came roaring back to deadlock the score. The game, which was back and forth, was exciting and nerve-racking, especially if you were a fan of one of the teams. We were anxious the entire game. Stanford was driving late in the game and running out the clock but missed a late chip shot field goal to seal the victory. The game went into overtime. Stanford went on offense and missed another short field goal. When OSU got the ball, they drove to the one yard line and kicked a field goal, pulling out the victory in dramatic fashion. The Stanford fans were stunned, but we were elated. The celebration lingered for hours.

When we got back to our room later that night, my sons and I turned on the television, and the channel was replaying the game we had just finished watching a few hours earlier. That's pretty incredible to watch a replay that quickly. We sat down to watch it, and I have to say that I was much more relaxed watching the replay. Even when OSU fell behind 14–0 and several other times, I wasn't panicked. No sweat. Why? I already knew the outcome. I knew that we won.

None of the setbacks, turnovers, or missed opportunities caused me the least bit of anxiety. I knew how it would finally end. I even went to bed before the replay was over.[4]

There's something about knowing the outcome in advance that brings us peace and rest. The same should be true of our lives now. While we don't know every detail of what's ahead, we do know who wins. The final score is already in the Book. Knowing what's ahead gives us hope, comfort, and confidence in a troubled, uncertain world.

Our world today is awash in anxiety and drowning in discouragement. There's a collective angst that things are spinning out of control. People everywhere today seem more downcast, discouraged, demoralized, and even depressed than ever before. On almost every front the news is dark: international unrest, domestic uncertainty, and even personal and family struggles. Yet in spite of the seemingly unending Niagara of bad news, God's people have hope. Praise God, we know the end of the story. God has given us glimpses of the future—rays of hope—to reassure us that He is in total control.

As you face the future—your future—remember that God is in total control. He is the Creator of the heavens and the earth. He alone knows the future. As Philip De Courcy says, "God has His providential Hand on the tiller of history. God's sovereignty is the Christian's North Star. Whatever is going on in this world, always remember that God, His Word, and His plan are still in their places."[5]

THE SON OF GOD

A second anchor point in uncertain times is the Son of God. Someday Jesus will come to take us to be with Himself. Jesus gave this promise in John 14:1-3. "Do not let your heart be troubled; believe in God, believe also in Me. In My Father's house are many dwelling places; if it were not so, I would have told you; for I go to prepare a place for you. If I go and prepare a place for you, I will come again and receive you to Myself, that where I am, there you may be also." In these verses three points are emphasized—a Person, a place, and a promise. The Person is Jesus, the place is heaven, and the promise is that He will come again someday to take His people there. We need to keep our eyes on Him.

Jean François Gravelet, the Great Blondin, was a master tightrope walker. On June 30, 1859, he was the first person to cross the yawning gorge of the Niagara River on a tightrope. Someone once asked him, "How do you manage to do that without falling?" He said, "Go and look on the other side in the direction in which I am walking. Do you see that silver star? I placed it there. I never take my eyes off of it. I put my eyes on that star, and I walk toward it. That's what gives me stability."[6] Jesus is our ultimate fixed reference point. Looking at Jesus, who is our Bright and Morning Star, will give you stability and peace of mind.

I read somewhere that Corrie ten Boom once said, "Look at the world, and you'll get distressed. Look within, and you'll get depressed. Look at Jesus, and you'll find rest."

That's excellent advice. What's more, it's biblical wisdom. Keep your eyes focused on Him. He never moves.

THE SALVATION OF GOD

The third reference point God has given us is His gracious salvation and forgiveness through Jesus Christ, who died for us and offers us the free gift of eternal life. God is our Sovereign, but He's also our Savior. I love the story Dr. David Jeremiah relates about Old Man Klein. Mr. Klein had lived life for himself, and his wicked life had left him old, miserable, and alone. He never attended church because, despite his self-serving life, he was all too aware of the many sins he had committed.

But it happened that as he walked by a church one Sunday evening, he heard people singing hymns, and this singing brought to mind his own loneliness. He stopped by the door to better listen to the music. He recognized the tune, but he had never before considered the hymn's words:

Saved by grace alone
This is all my plea,
Jesus died for Old Man Klein,
And Jesus died for me.

He couldn't believe his ears. Was this possible? The hymn had mentioned him by name, and all the people were singing as if nothing was out of place. He had to investigate, and he slipped into the back pew. Mr. Klein was deeply moved—the gospel wasn't just for others; it was for him. But he still wondered—how could the song name him so specifically? He turned in the hymnbook to find the song, and the words he had heard were actually "Jesus died for all mankind."

Or were they?

Old Man Klein laughed. It didn't matter if he had misheard. After all, "all mankind" includes even "Old Man Klein."[7]

"All mankind" includes you, too. Jesus died for you. He died in your place as your substitute. No matter what you've done, you can come to Jesus and be forgiven of all your sins and receive the free gift of eternal life. If you've never done so, why not trust Christ right now? Accept His sacrifice for your sins and take Him to be your Savior. John 1:12 says, "As many as received Him, to them He gave the right to become children of God, even to those who believe in His name." Jesus died in your place on the cross and purchased a full, free pardon for you from all your sins. Accept that pardon now, and allow these immovable anchor points to secure your life—the sovereignty of God, the Son of God, and the salvation of God.

SHINING IN THE DARKNESS

On May 19, 1780, many people in New England thought that the Day of the Lord had arrived when the sky inexplicably became pitch black during the day. The darkness was not due to an eclipse since the moon was almost full. It also was not caused by clouds or the thickness of the atmosphere. In some places where the darkness settled, the sky was so clear that the stars could be seen.

The extent of the darkness was remarkable. It was observed at the farthest eastern regions of New England; westward it spread to the farthest part of Connecticut; southward at Albany, it was observed all along the seacoast; and to the north, the land was blanketed in darkness as far as the American settlements extended. It probably far exceeded those boundaries, but the exact limits were never positively known. The duration of the darkness was substantial, continuing in the neighborhood of Boston for at least fourteen or fifteen hours.

During that dark day in 1780, the House of Representatives was convened in Hartford, Connecticut, under the leadership of its speaker, Colonel Abraham Davenport. The steady resolve of Abraham Davenport during this troubling time is described by Timothy Dwight of Yale in his *Travels in New England and New York*, published in 1822:

The 19th of May, 1780, was a remarkably dark day. Candles were lighted in many houses; the birds were silent and disappeared; and the fowls retired to roost. The legislature of Connecticut was then in session at Hartford. A very general opinion prevailed that the Day of Judgment was at hand. The House of Representatives, being unable to transact their business, adjourned. A proposal to adjourn the Council [Senate or Upper House] was under consideration. When the opinion of Col. Davenport was asked, he answered, "I am against an adjournment. The Day of Judgment is either approaching, or it is not. If it is not, there is no cause for an adjournment; if it is, I choose to be found doing my duty. I wish therefore that candles may be brought."[8]

As our world grows darker, literally and spiritually, and some are heralding the darkening of the sun and the moon as omens of disaster, we should follow the example of Abraham Davenport by bringing in the candles and shining in the darkness as we keep laboring for our Lord until He comes.

Maranatha! May He come soon!

LEVITICUS 23: THE FEASTS OF THE LORD

THE LORD SPOKE again to Moses, saying, "Speak to the sons of Israel and say to them, 'The LORD's appointed times which you shall proclaim as holy convocations—My appointed times are these: 'For six days work may be done, but on the seventh day there is a sabbath of complete rest, a holy convocation. You shall not do any work; it is a sabbath to the LORD in all your dwellings. These are the appointed times of the LORD, holy convocations which you shall proclaim at the times appointed for them. In the first month, on the fourteenth day of the month at twilight is the LORD's Passover. Then on the fifteenth day of the same month there is the Feast of Unleavened Bread to the LORD; for seven days you shall eat unleavened bread. On the first day you shall have a holy convocation; you shall not do any laborious work. But for seven days you shall present an offering by fire to the LORD. On the seventh day is a holy convocation; you shall not do any laborious work.'"

Then the LORD spoke to Moses, saying, "Speak to the

sons of Israel and say to them, 'When you enter the land which I am going to give to you and reap its harvest, then you shall bring in the sheaf of the first fruits of your harvest to the priest. He shall wave the sheaf before the LORD for you to be accepted; on the day after the sabbath the priest shall wave it. Now on the day when you wave the sheaf, you shall offer a male lamb one year old without defect for a burnt offering to the LORD. Its grain offering shall then be two-tenths of an ephah of fine flour mixed with oil, an offering by fire to the LORD for a soothing aroma, with its drink offering, a fourth of a hin of wine. Until this same day, until you have brought in the offering of your God, you shall eat neither bread nor roasted grain nor new growth. It is to be a perpetual statute throughout your generations in all your dwelling places.

'You shall also count for yourselves from the day after the sabbath, from the day when you brought in the sheaf of the wave offering; there shall be seven complete sabbaths. You shall count fifty days to the day after the seventh sabbath; then you shall present a new grain offering to the LORD. You shall bring in from your dwelling places two loaves of bread for a wave offering, made of two-tenths of an ephah; they shall be of a fine flour, baked with leaven as first fruits to the LORD. Along with the bread you shall present seven one year old male lambs without defect, and a bull of the herd and two rams; they are to be a burnt offering to the LORD, with their grain offering and their drink offerings, an offering by fire of a soothing aroma to the LORD. You shall also offer one male goat for a sin offering and two male lambs one year old for a sacrifice of peace offerings. The priest shall then wave them with the bread of the first fruits for a wave offering with two lambs before the LORD; they are to be holy to the LORD for the priest. On this same day you shall make a proclamation as well; you are to have a holy convocation. You shall do no laborious work. It is to be a perpetual statute in all your dwelling places throughout your generations. When you reap the harvest of your land, moreover, you shall not reap to the very corners of your field nor gather the gleaning of your harvest; you are to leave them for the needy and the alien. I am the LORD your God.'"

Again the LORD spoke to Moses, saying, "Speak to the sons of Israel, saying, 'In the seventh month on the first of the month you shall have a rest, a reminder by blowing of trumpets, a holy convocation. You shall not do any laborious work, but you shall present an offering by fire to the LORD.'"

The LORD spoke to Moses, saying, "On exactly the tenth day of this seventh month is the day of atonement; it shall be a holy convocation for you, and you shall humble your souls and present an offering by fire to the LORD. You shall not do any work on this same day, for it is a day of atonement, to make atonement on your behalf before the LORD your God. If there is any person who will not humble himself on this same day, he shall be cut off from his people. As for any person who does any work on this same day, that person I will destroy from among his people. You shall do no work at all. It is to be a perpetual statute throughout your generations in all your dwelling places. It is to be a sabbath of complete rest to you, and you shall humble your souls; on the ninth of the month at evening, from evening until evening you shall keep your sabbath."

Again the LORD spoke to Moses, saying, "Speak to the sons of Israel, saying, 'On the fifteenth of this seventh month is the Feast of Booths for seven days to the LORD. On the first day is a holy convocation; you shall do no laborious work of any kind. For seven days you shall present an offering by fire to the LORD. On the eighth day you shall have a holy convocation and present an offering by fire to the LORD; it is an assembly. You shall do no laborious work.

'These are the appointed times of the LORD which you shall proclaim as holy convocations, to present offerings by fire to the LORD—burnt offerings and grain offerings, sacrifices and drink offerings, each day's matter on its own day—besides those of the sabbaths of the LORD, and besides your gifts and besides all your votive and freewill offerings, which you give to the LORD.

'On exactly the fifteenth day of the seventh month, when you have gathered in the crops of the land, you shall celebrate the feast of the LORD for seven days, with a rest on the first day and a rest on the eighth day. Now on the first day you shall take for yourselves the foliage of beautiful trees, palm branches and boughs of leafy trees and willows of the brook, and you shall rejoice before the LORD your God for seven days. You shall thus celebrate it as a feast to the LORD for seven days in the year. It shall be a perpetual statute throughout your generations; you shall celebrate it in the seventh month. You shall live in booths for seven days; all the native-born in Israel shall live in booths, so that your generations may know that I had the sons of Israel live in booths when I brought them out from the land of Egypt. I am the LORD your God.'" So Moses declared to the sons of Israel the appointed times of the LORD.

Appendix 2

FORESHADOWS
OF THE FUTURE

NO ONE KNOWS the time when Jesus will come, or the date of any other end-times event. Jesus made that crystal clear. Yet Jesus did give a set of startling signs in Matthew 24:4-31 that will portend His coming. Jesus was *against* setting dates, but He was *for* signs of the times. So, if the blood moons prophecy is not a valid sign of the times, what are some discernible signs that we've witnessed in the last few decades? What are some of the foreshadows of the future?

In a book that I had the privilege to coauthor with Dr. John Walvoord, titled *Armageddon, Oil, and Terror*, we provided a fairly extensive list of signposts that line the road to Armageddon. I've included these lists here for you to consider in light of what's happening today. The signs and future events are divided into three streams that are merging into one raging river: signs related to the church, signs related to the nations, and signs related to Israel.

A PROPHETIC CHECKLIST
FOR THE CHURCH

When all the predicted events relating to the church are placed in chronological order, it is evident that the world has already been carefully prepared for Christ's return. This checklist includes the major prophetic events in the order of their predicted fulfillment.

1. The rise of world communism makes possible the worldwide spread of atheism.
2. Liberalism undermines and saps the spiritual vitality of the church in Europe and eventually America.
3. The movement toward a superchurch or amalgamation of Christendom begins with the ecumenical movement.
4. Apostasy, which means falling away from or standing against the truth, and open denial of biblical truth are evident and escalating dramatically in the church.
5. Moral chaos becomes more and more evident and even accepted and promoted because of the complete departure from Christian morality that results from the departure from Christian theology.
6. The sweep of spiritism, the occult, and belief in demons begins to prepare the world for Satan's final hour.
7. Jerusalem becomes a center of religious controversy for Arabs and Christians, while Jews of the world plan to make the city an active center for Judaism.

8. True believers disappear from the earth to join Christ in heaven at the Rapture of the church, resulting in mass confusion.

9. The restraint of evil on earth by the Holy Spirit through the church is ended, opening the floodgates of evil.

10. The false superchurch combines major religions as a tool for the final false prophet, the end-times propagandist, who aids the Antichrist's rise to world power.

11. The Antichrist destroys the superchurch and demands worship as a deified world dictator.

12. Believers who come to Christ on earth after the Rapture suffer intense persecution and are martyred by the hundreds of thousands.

13. Christ returns to earth with Christians who have been in heaven during the Tribulation and ends the rule of the nations at the Battle of Armageddon.

A PROPHETIC CHECKLIST FOR THE NATIONS

The prophetic events related to the nations can be compiled chronologically. Consider how the following list of significant world events—past, present, and future—shows that the world is being dramatically prepared for end-times events.

1. The establishment of the League of Nations and then the United Nations began a serious first step toward world government.
2. The rebuilding of Europe after World War II made a revival of the Roman Empire possible.
3. Israel was reestablished as a nation in 1948.
4. Russia rose to world power and became the ally of the Islamic world.
5. The Common Market and World Bank showed the need for some international regulation of the world economy.
6. China rose to world power and developed the capacity to field an army of two hundred million as predicted in prophecy.[1]
7. The Middle East became the most significant trouble spot in the world.
8. The oil blackmail awakened the world to the new concentration of wealth and power in the Middle East and Persian Gulf.
9. The Iron Curtain fell, removing the final barrier to the revival of the Roman Empire.
10. The world clamors for peace because of the continued disruption caused by the high price of oil, terrorist incidents, and the confused military situation and chronic chaos in the Middle East.
11. After the Rapture, ten leaders (the "Group of Ten") will emerge from a European and Mediterranean Coalition—beginnings of the last stage of the

prophetic fourth world empire—the reunited Roman Empire.

12. In a dramatic power play, a new Mediterranean leader will uproot three leaders of the coalition and take control of the powerful ten-leader group.

13. The new Mediterranean leader will negotiate a "final" peace settlement in the Middle East (broken three and a half years later).

14. Russia and her Islamic allies will attempt an invasion of Israel but will be miraculously destroyed.

15. Filling the vacuum created by the destruction of the Russian-Islamic alliance, the Mediterranean leader will proclaim himself world dictator, break his peace settlement with Israel, and declare himself to be God.

16. The new world dictator will desecrate the Temple in Jerusalem. (This is the abomination of desolation.)

17. The three terrible waves of divine judgments of the Great Tribulation will be poured out on the nations of the world.

18. Worldwide rebellion will threaten the world dictator's rule as armies from throughout the world converge on the Middle East for World War III.

19. Christ will return to earth with His armies from heaven.

20. The armies of the world will unite to resist Christ's coming and will be destroyed in the Battle of Armageddon.

21. Christ will establish His millennial reign on earth, ending the time of the Gentiles.

A PROPHETIC CHECKLIST FOR ISRAEL

Although Israel's future cannot be separated from the wider sweep of history, prophecies about the Jewish people and the nation have their own distinct order of predicted events. In this prophetic checklist, as in the others, the events already in motion suggest the final countdown to Armageddon may already have begun.

1. The intense suffering and persecution of Jews throughout the world lead to pressure for a national home in Israel.
2. Jews return to the land, and Israel is reestablished as a nation in 1948.
3. The infant nation survives and thrives against overwhelming odds.
4. Russia emerges as an important enemy of Israel, but the United States stands with Israel and comes to its aid.
5. Israel's heroic survival and growing strength make it an established, formidable nation, recognized throughout the world.
6. Israel's military accomplishments are overshadowed by the Arabs' ability to wage a diplomatic war by controlling much of the world's oil reserves.

7. The Arab position is strengthened by their growing wealth and by alliances between Europe and key Arab countries.

8. The increasing alienation of the United States from the Middle East makes it more and more difficult for Israel to negotiate an acceptable peace settlement.

9. Israel finds itself more and more isolated and alone on the world political and diplomatic stage.

10. After a long struggle, Israel will be forced to accept a compromise peace guaranteed by the new leader of the European and Mediterranean Union.

11. The Jewish people will celebrate what appears to be a lasting and final peace settlement.

12. During three and a half years of peace, Judaism will be revived and traditional sacrifices and ceremonies reinstituted in the rebuilt Temple in Jerusalem.

13. Russia and its Islamic allies will attempt to invade Israel but will be mysteriously destroyed.

14. The newly proclaimed world dictator will desecrate the Temple in Jerusalem and begin a period of intense persecution of Jews.

15. Many Jews will recognize the unfolding of prophetic events and declare their faith in Christ as the Messiah of Israel.

16. In the massacre of Jews and Christians who resist the world dictator, some witnesses will be divinely preserved to carry the gospel message throughout the world.

17. Christ will return to earth, welcomed by believing Jews as their Messiah and Deliverer.

18. Christ's thousand-year reign on earth from the throne of David will finally fulfill the covenant promises to the nation of Israel (the Abrahamic Covenant, Land Covenant, Davidic Covenant, and New Covenant).

The earth appears to be on the verge of entering into its most dangerous and difficult days. Events in our world today strikingly foreshadow the end-times prophecies of Scripture. No one knows the time, but based on what we see, time may be very short.

A PROPOSED CHRONOLOGY OF THE END TIMES

IN MANY OF my books on end-times prophecy I like to include this outline at the end.[1] It's not easy to fit together all the pieces of the end times into a chronological sequence. This outline is my best attempt to put the pieces together. I don't insist on the correctness of every detail in this outline, but my prayer is that it will help you get a better grasp of the overall flow of events in the end times.

I. EVENTS IN HEAVEN

A. *The Rapture of the Church (1 Cor. 15:51-58; 1 Thess. 4:13-18; Rev. 3:10)*

B. *The Judgment Seat of Christ (Rom. 14:10; 1 Cor. 3:9-15; 4:1-5; 9:24-27; 2 Cor. 5:10)*

C. *The Marriage of the Lamb (2 Cor. 11:2; Rev. 19:6-8)*

D. *The Singing of Two Special Songs (Rev. 4–5)*

E. *The Lamb Receiving the Seven-Sealed Scroll (Rev. 5)*

II. EVENTS ON EARTH

A. Seven-Year Tribulation

    1. Beginning of the Tribulation

        a. Seven-year Tribulation begins when the Antichrist signs a covenant with Israel, bringing peace to Israel and Jerusalem (Dan. 9:27; Ezek. 38:8, 11).

        b. The Jewish Temple in Jerusalem is rebuilt (Dan. 9:27; Rev. 11:1).

        c. The reunited Roman Empire emerges in a ten-nation confederation (Dan. 2:40-44; 7:7; Rev. 17:12).

    2. First Half (Three and a Half Years) of the Tribulation

        a. The seven seal judgments are opened (Rev. 6).

        b. The 144,000 Jewish believers begin their great evangelistic ministry (Rev. 7).

        c. Gog and his allies invade Israel, while Israel is at peace under the covenant with Antichrist, and are supernaturally decimated by God (Daniel 11:40-45; Ezek. 38–39). This will probably occur somewhere near the end of the three-and-a-half-year period. The destruction of these forces will create a major shift in the balance of power that will enable the Antichrist to begin his rise to world ascendancy.

    3. The Midpoint of the Tribulation

        a. Antichrist breaks his covenant with Israel and invades the land (Dan. 9:27; 11:40-41).

b. Antichrist begins to consolidate his empire by plundering Egypt, Sudan, and Libya, whose armies have just been destroyed by God in Israel (Dan. 11:42-43; Ezek. 38–39).

c. While in North Africa, Antichrist hears disturbing news of insurrection in Israel and immediately returns there to destroy and annihilate many (Dan. 11:44).

d. Antichrist sets up the abomination of desolation in the rebuilt Temple in Jerusalem (Dan. 9:27; 11:45; Matt. 24:15; 2 Thess. 2:4; Rev. 13:5, 15-18).

e. Sometime during these events, the Antichrist is violently killed, possibly as a result of a war or assassination (Dan. 11:45; Rev. 13:3, 12, 14; 17:8).

f. Satan is cast down from heaven and begins to make war with the woman, Israel (Rev. 12:7-13). The chief means he uses to persecute Israel is the two beasts in Revelation 13.

g. The faithful Jewish remnant flee to Petra in modern Jordan, where they are divinely protected for the remainder of the Tribulation (Matt. 24:16-20; Rev. 12:15-17).

h. The Antichrist is miraculously raised from the dead to the awestruck amazement of the entire world (Rev. 13:3).

i. After his resurrection from the dead, the Antichrist gains political control over the ten kings of the reunited Roman empire. Three of these kings will be killed by the Antichrist and the other seven will submit (Dan. 7:24; Rev. 17:12-13).

j. The two witnesses begin their three-and-a-half-year ministry (Rev. 11:2-3).

k. Antichrist and the ten kings destroy the religious system of Babylon and set up their religious capital in the city (Revelation 17:16-17).

4. Last Half (Three and a Half Years) of the Tribulation

a. Antichrist blasphemes God, and the false prophet performs great signs and wonders and promotes false worship of the Antichrist (Rev. 13:5, 11-15).

b. The mark of the beast (666) is introduced and enforced by the false prophet (Rev. 13:16-18).

c. Totally energized by Satan, the Antichrist dominates the world politically, religiously, and economically (Rev. 13:4-5, 15-18).

d. The trumpet judgments are unleashed throughout the final half of the Tribulation (Rev. 8–9).

e. Knowing he has only a short time left, Satan intensifies his relentless, merciless persecution of the Jewish people and Gentile believers on earth (Dan. 7:25; Rev. 12:12; 13:15; 20:4).

5. The End of the Tribulation

a. The bowl judgments are poured out in rapid succession (Rev. 16).

b. The Campaign of Armageddon begins (Rev. 16:16).

    c. Commercial Babylon is destroyed (Rev. 18).

    d. The two witnesses are killed by Antichrist and are resurrected by God three and a half days later (Rev. 11:7-12).

    e. Christ returns to the Mount of Olives and slays the armies gathered against Him throughout the land, from Megiddo to Petra (Rev. 19:11-16; Isa. 34:1-6; 63:1-5).

    f. The birds gather to feed on the carnage (Rev. 19:17-18).

B. *After the Tribulation*

1. Interval or Transition Period of Seventy-Five days (Dan. 12:12)

    a. The Antichrist and the false prophet are cast in the lake of fire (Rev. 19:20-21).

    b. The abomination of desolation is removed from the Temple (Dan. 12:11).

    c. Israel is regathered (Matt. 24:31).

    d. Israel is judged (Ezek. 20:30-39; Matt. 25:1-30).

    e. Gentiles are judged (Matt. 25:31-46).

    f. Satan is bound in the abyss (Rev. 20:1-3).

    g. OT and Tribulation saints are resurrected (Dan. 12:1-3; Isa. 26:19; Rev. 20:4).

2. One-Thousand-Year Reign of Christ on Earth (Rev. 20:4-6)

3. Satan's Final Revolt and Defeat (Rev. 20:7-10)

4. The Great White Throne Judgment of the Lost
   (Rev. 20:11-15)
5. The Destruction of the Present Heavens and Earth
   (Matt. 24:35; 2 Pet. 3:3-12; Rev. 21:1)
6. The Creation of the New Heavens and New Earth
   (Isa. 65:17; 66:22; 2 Pet. 3:13; Rev. 21:1)
7. Eternity (Rev. 21:9–22:5)

NOTES

EPIGRAPH

1. John Hagee, *Four Blood Moons: Something Is about to Change* (Brentwood, TN: Worthy Publishing, 2013), 25, 51, 237.

CHAPTER ONE: THE FINAL FOUR?

1. Billy Graham, *The Reason for My Hope: Salvation* (Nashville, TN: W Publishing Group, 2013), 173, 175.
2. Alfred North Whitehead, *Science and the Modern World* (New York; Cambridge University Press, 1926), 259.
3. Heather Warlick, "World's Largest Private Underground Shelter Being Built in Kansas" *The Oklahoman*, October 22, 2013, http://newsok.com /worlds-largest-private-underground-shelter-being-built-in-kansas/article /3896504.
4. Arthur C. Clarke, quoted in Richard A. Swenson, *Hurtling toward Oblivion: A Logical Argument for the End of the Age* (Colorado Springs: NavPress, 1999), 20.
5. Jeremy Weber, "Survey Surprise: Many Americans See Syria as Sign of Bible's End Times," *Christianity Today*, September 13, 2013, www.christianitytoday .com/gleanings/2013/september/syria-survey-end-times-armageddon-lifeway .html.
6. Swenson, *Hurtling toward Oblivion*, 19–20.
7. Hagee, *Four Blood Moons*, 237, 244.
8. Michael Snyder, "The Blood Red Moons of 2014 and 2015: An Omen of War for Israel?", *The Truth*, September 2, 2013, www.thetruthwins.com /archives/the-blood-red-moons-of-2014-and-2015-an.
9. Hagee, *Four Blood Moons*, 51.

CHAPTER TWO: SETTING THE STAGE

1   John F. Walvoord, *Armageddon, Oil, and the Middle East Crisis*, rev. ed. (Grand Rapids, MI: Zondervan, 1990), 22.

2. "Actual Signs That We Have Found," Bored.com, www.bored.com /signhumor.

3. Thomas Ice and Timothy Demy, *The Truth about the Signs of the Times* (Eugene, OR: Harvest House Publishers, 1997), 13.

4. Swenson, *Hurtling toward Oblivion*, 15–16.

5. For an excellent discussion of the difference between facts, assumptions, and speculations, see Ed Hindson, *Final Signs: Amazing Prophecies of the End Times* (Eugene, OR: Harvest House Publishers, 1996), 36–37.

6. Walvoord, *Armageddon, Oil, and the Middle East Crisis*, 217.

7. Ice and Demy, *The Truth about the Signs of the Times*, 10–11.

8. Thomas Ice, "Signs of the Times and Prophetic Fulfillment," www.raptureready.com/featured/ice/SignsoftheTimesandProphetic Fulfillment.html

9. Swenson, *Hurtling toward Oblivion*, 54.

10. John F. Walvoord, *The Return of the Lord* (Findlay, OH: Dunham Publishing Company, 1955), 16–17.

11. I also used this illustration in *Iran and Israel* (Eugene, OR: Harvest House Publishers, 2013), www.harvesthousepublishers.com. Used by permission.

12. This story, adapted from Donald Grey Barnhouse, is related by James Montgomery Boice, *The Last and Future World* (Grand Rapids, MI: Zondervan, 1974), 49–50.

13. Walvoord, *Armageddon, Oil, and the Middle East Crisis*, 228.

CHAPTER THREE: THE END-TIMES SCRIPT

1. Amiram Barkat, "Statistics Bureau: Israeli Jews Outnumber Jews in the U.S.," Haaretz.com, June 17, 2003, www.haaretz.com/print-edition /news/statistics-bureau-israeli-jews-outnumber-jews-in-the-u-s-1.91466.

2. Adrian Rogers, *Unveiling the End Times in Our Time* (Nashville, TN: B&H, 2004), 142.

3. The reason I refer to nineteen judgments instead of twenty-one is that the seventh seal contains the seven trumpets and the seventh trumpet contains the seven bowls.

4. Graham, *The Reason for My Hope*, 176.

5. These twenty prophecies are adapted from John F. Walvoord, *Prophecy Knowledge Handbook* (Wheaton, IL: Victor Books).

CHAPTER FOUR: DARK SIDE OF THE MOON

1. Laura Motel, "A Busy Day On the Celestial Calendar: A Total Lunar Eclipse and the Winter Solstice Coincide on December 21," *NASA*, December 17, 2010, www.nasa.gov/topics/solarsystem/features/eclipse /dec21-eclipse.html.

2. Hagee, *Four Blood Moons*, 20.

3. Ibid.

4. Richard A. Swenson, *More Than Meets the Eye* (Colorado Springs: NavPress, 2000), 158.

5. Bary Alyssa Johnson, "Skywatching Calendar of Events 2014: Total Lunar Eclipses, Supermoon, Meteor Showers, Possible Collision Between Comet and Mars & More," *Latin Post*, December 30, 2013, www.latinpost.com /articles/5303/20131230/skywatching-calendar-of-events-2014-two-lunar -eclipses-supermoon-meteor-showers-possible-collision-between-comet -and-mars-stargazing-more.htm.

6. "Lunar Eclipse Calendar," *Moon Giant*, www.moongiant.com/Lunar _Eclipse_Calendar.php.

7. Hagee, *Four Blood Moons*, 45.

8. Ibid., 225.

9. Ibid., 51.

CHAPTER FIVE: SEVEN FEASTS AND FOUR BLOOD MOONS

1. Warren W. Wiersbe, *The Wiersbe Bible Commentary*, Old Testament (Colorado Springs: David C. Cook, 2007), 235.

2. Ray C. Stedman, *The Way to Wholeness: Lessons from Leviticus* (Grand Rapids, MI: Discovery House, 2005), 251–252.

3. F. Duane Lindsey, "Leviticus," in *The Bible Knowledge Commentary*, ed. John F. Walvoord and Roy B. Zuck (Wheaton, IL: Victor Books, 1985), 163.

4. Wiersbe, *The Wiersbe Bible Commentary*, 237.

5. A. Noordtzij, "Leviticus," in *Bible Student's Commentary*, translated by Raymond Togtman (Grand Rapids, MI: Zondervan, 1982), 231.

6. I follow the chronology laid out by Harold W. Hoehner, *Chronological Aspects of the Life of Christ* (Grand Rapids, MI: Zondervan, 1977), 65–113.

7. Stedman, *The Way to Wholeness*, 262.

8. Arnold Fruchtenbaum, *A Review of Marvin Rosenthal's Book "The Pre-Wrath Rapture of the Church"* (Tustin, CA: Ariel Ministries, 1991), 58.

9. Thomas Ice, "Israel's Fall Feasts and Date-Setting of the Rapture," Pre-Trib Research Center, www.pre-trib.org/articles/ view/israels-fall-feasts-and-date-setting-of-rapture.

10. R. Laird Harris, "Leviticus," in *The Expositor's Bible Commentary*, ed. Frank E. Gaebelein, vol. 2 (Grand Rapids, MI: Zondervan, 1990), 628.

11. Wiersbe, *The Wiersbe Bible Commentary*, 238.

12. Harris, "Leviticus," 629.

13. Wiersbe, *The Wiersbe Bible Commentary*, 238.

14. William MacDonald, *Believer's Bible Commentary*, Old Testament (Nashville: Thomas Nelson Publishers, 1992), 161.

CHAPTER SIX: MOONSHINE: SIGNS IN THE HEAVENS

1. Swenson, *More Than Meets the Eye*, 158.

2. Ibid., 144.

3. Ibid., 158.

4. Hagee, *Four Blood Moons*, 20.

5. Jack Kelley, "The Coming Blood Moons," *Rapture Ready*, www.raptureready.com/featured/kelley/jack274.html.

6. Dr. Danny R. Faulkner, "Will Lunar Eclipses Cause Four Blood Moons in 2014 and 2015?" AnswersinGenesis.org, July 12, 2013, www.answersingenesis.org/articles/2013/07/12/lunar-eclipses-cause-blood-moons.

7. Fred Espenak, "Eclipses During 2014," NASA Eclipse Web Site, http://eclipse.gsfc.nasa.gov/OH/OH2014.html.

8. Ibid.

9. Kelley, "The Coming Blood Moons."

10. See D. A. Carson, "Matthew," in *The Expositor's Bible Commentary*, gen. ed. Frank E. Gaebelein, vol. 8 (Grand Rapids, MI: Zondervan Publishing House, 1984), 85.

11. R. C. Sproul, *Matthew*, St. Andrew's Expositional Commentary (Wheaton, IL: Crossway, 2013), 29.

12. John MacArthur, *The MacArthur New Testament Commentary: Matthew 1–7* (Chicago: Moody Press, 1985), 29–30. John Walvoord suggests another plausible interpretation: "One intriguing possibility is that the original sign in the sky seen by the wise men could have been the angelic choir that appeared to the shepherds the night of Jesus' birth. In the Old Testament angels were pictured as stars (Job 38:7; Isa. 14:12-13). The glow in the night sky that night must have been visible for miles, perhaps for hundreds of miles. And the reappearance of an angel could then be the 'star' that guided the wise men to Bethlehem, and to the very house where Jesus and his parents were staying." John F. Walvoord and Charles H. Dyer, ed. Philip E. Rawley, *Matthew* (Chicago: Moody Publishers, 2013), 35.

CHAPTER SEVEN: BLOOD MOONS AND BIBLE PROPHECY

1. Paul Lee Tan, *The Interpretation of Prophecy* (Winona Lake, IN: Assurance Publishers, 1974), 29.
2. Jesus didn't distinguish the timing of the destruction of Jerusalem (AD 70) from the events of the end times because He knew their main question was about the signals of His return to earth.
3. Hagee, *Four Blood Moons*, 44.
4. Leon Morris, *The Gospel According to Matthew* (Grand Rapids, MI: Wm. B. Eerdmans Publishing Co., 1992), 609.

CHAPTER EIGHT: ONCE IN A BLOOD MOON

1. "Blood Moons: Christians 'on Wrong Calendar,'" WorldNetDaily, October 16, 2013, www.wnd.com/2013/10/blood-moons-christians -on-wrong-calendar/#AH5JOhiYogAfM3TS.99.
2. Some prophecy teachers have identified previous blood moon tetrads and aligned them with important events that occurred for Israel. However, since John Hagee has popularized this view and discusses only the three previous tetrads of 1493–1494, 1949–1950, and 1967–1968, I've limited my scope to these three exclusively.
3. "The Edict of the Expulsion of the Jews," *Foundation for the Advancement of Sephardic Studies and Culture*, trans. Edward Peters, www.sephardicstudies .org/decree.html.
4. Hagee, *Four Blood Moons*, 195.

CHAPTER NINE: THE DATING GAME

1. C. S. Lewis, "Is Progress Possible?" *God in the Dock: Essays on Theology and Ethics* (Grand Rapids, MI: Eerdmans, 1970), 312.
2. This is adapted from Robert J. Morgan, *On This Day in Christian History* (Nashville: Thomas Nelson, 1997), October 22.
3. J. Gregory Sheryl, "Can the Date of Jesus' Return Be Known?" *Bibliotheca Sacra* 169 (January–March 2012): 27.
4. Ibid.
5. Hagee, *Four Blood Moons*, 234.
6. Ibid., 237.
7. For other examples, see Hal Lindsey, *The Late Great Planet Earth* (Grand Rapids, MI: Zondervan, 1970), 53–54, and Jack Van Impe, "A Message of Hope from Dr. Jack Van Impe," *Jack Van Impe Ministries*, www.jvim.com /newsletter/pastissues/2012/20121022.html.
8. Hagee, *Four Blood Moons*, 229.
9. Ibid., 228.

10. John MacArthur, *The MacArthur New Testament Commentary: Matthew 24–28* (Chicago: Moody Press, 1989), 61.

11. John F. Walvoord and Charles H. Dyer, *Matthew,* ed. Philip E. Rawley (Chicago: Moody Publishers, 2013), 329.

12. Ibid., 330.

13. Warren W. Wiersbe, *The Bible Exposition Commentary*, vol. 2 (Wheaton, IL: Victor Books, 1989), 196.

14. Sheryl, "Can the Date of Jesus' Return Be Known?," 48.

15. Ed Hindson, *Final Signs: Amazing Prophecies of the End Times* (Eugene, OR: Harvest House Publishers, 1996), 196.

CHAPTER TEN: BLOOD MOONS AND YOU

1. Swenson, *Hurtling toward Oblivion*, 17.

2. Walvoord, *The Return of the Lord*, 17.

3. Maunsell B. Field, *Memories of Many Men and of Some Women* (New York: Harper and Brothers, 1874), 313.

4. I also used this illustration in *Iran and Israel* (Eugene, OR: Harvest House Publishers, 2013), www.harvesthousepublishers.com. Used by permission.

5. Philip De Courcy, *Truth Matters* (Anaheim, CA: Know the Truth, 2013), 53.

6. Rogers, *Unveiling the End Times in Our Time*, 2004), 8.

7. David Jeremiah, *God Loves You* (New York: FaithWords, 2012), 129–30.

8. Timothy Dwight in "Bring in the Candles," *The Thicket at State Legislatures,* March 24, 2010, ncsl.typepad.com/the_thicket/2010/03 /bring-in-the-candles.html.

APPENDIX 2: FORESHADOWS OF THE FUTURE

1. I believe the army of two hundred million in Revelation 9:13-21 is a demonic horde that is unleashed to kill one-third of the earth's inhabitants. Dr. Walvoord and many others believe Revelation 9 prophesies a massive human army that will be part of the Campaign of Armageddon. Either view is possible.

APPENDIX 3: A PROPOSED CHRONOLOGY OF THE END TIMES

1. This chronology was adapted from my book *The Complete Book of Bible Prophecy* (Wheaton, IL: Tyndale House, 1999), 229–31.

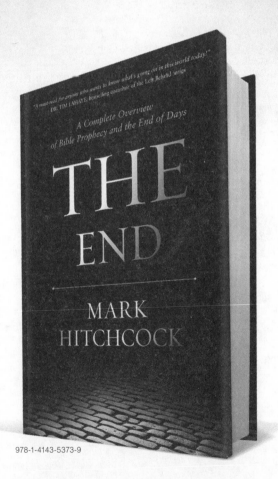